Official Game Guide
Written by David Knight

To redeem your **FREE** eGuide, enter the code below at primagames.com/code

AC8E-W5BT-M299-S4M2

FREE UPDATES
Coverage of brand new content is included—watch for new maps and game modes as they're released!

PORTABLE
Access your eGuide on any device with an Internet connection.

SEARCHABLE
Quickly find everything you need!

2

WELCOME TO INKOPOLIS

Welcome to the official game guide for *Splatoon*. Whether spreading ink in online Turf War matches or splatting Octarians in the single-player campaign, *Splatoon* offers a unique take on the third-person action shooter. Strategy is key as you guide your Inkling through each stage, using your ink to secure territory for your team. While the objectives and gameplay mechanics are easy to learn, the game's deep progression and customization systems help keep players engaged as they level up and outfit their Inkling with new weapons and gear. Get ready for hours of exciting and addictive gameplay as you make a name for yourself in Inkopolis' competitive ink battle scene.

GETTING STARTED

Inkling Creation

In *Splatoon*, you assume the role of an Inkling, a humanoid-squid hybrid. When first starting the game, you're prompted to choose a girl or boy Inkling—this is the character you'll play as during the single-player campaign as well as online matches. Your Inkling's gender is purely aesthetic and has no bearing on how your character performs. The same is true for your Inkling's skin tone and eye color, two other attributes

Choose your Inkling's gender as well as their skin tone and eye color.

you're prompted to select. Later on, you can further customize your Inkling by outfitting them with different clothing, shoes, and headgear—these items can enhance your Inkling's performance. But for now, you'll need to make do with the standard-issue Basic Tee, Cream Basics, and White Headband.

Controls

ZL: Squid Form

Move

Sub Weapon Selection

ZR: Shoot Ink

R: Throw Sub Weapon

Look/ Activate Special

Jump

Reset Camera

Motion Controls

By default, motion controls are active, allowing you to aim by tilting the GamePad up and down. If you prefer to use the Right Analog Stick to aim, turn off motion controls in the Control Settings under the GamePad's Options menu.

Tutorial: The Path to Inkopolis

During the tutorial, experiment with swimming and jumping while in squid form. Mastering these skills is essential for surviving ink battles.

After personalizing your Inkling, you're immediately ushered in to a quick tutorial, giving you a chance to familiarize yourself with the game's controls in a hostile-free environment. Advance through this stage while popping balloons and spreading ink. There's no rush, so take some time to experiment with the game's unique gameplay mechanics. For example, spread ink across horizontal and vertical surfaces, then swim through your ink in squid form—while swimming through your ink, your ink tank replenishes at a much faster rate. Swimming through ink also makes you more difficult to detect, allowing you to sneak past enemies. Also, get familiar with the Splat Bombs. Hold down the R Button to see the bomb's trajectory before throwing—this allows for more precise targeting, particularly when throwing a Splat Bomb from behind cover. When you feel comfortable with the game's controls and mechanics, continue to the launchpad at the end of the stage. Stand on the launchpad and press the ZL Button to perform a Super Jump, taking you all the way to Inkopolis Plaza.

INKOPOLIS PLAZA: POINTS OF INTEREST

After completing the tutorial, you land in the center of Inkopolis Plaza, a bustling hub of activity for Inklings obsessed with ink battles. Turn your attention to the overhead monitor for the latest broadcast of Inkopolis News, hosted by Callie and Marie—apparently the Great Zapfish is missing from Inkopolis Tower. Could this be connected with the recent UFO sightings? In any case, Callie and Marie don't seem too worried about this latest development. Following the broadcast, feel free to explore the Plaza—there's plenty to see and do.

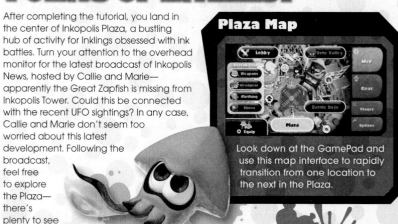

Plaza Map

Look down at the GamePad and use this map interface to rapidly transition from one location to the next in the Plaza.

Inkopolis Tower

Enter the lobby at the base of Inkopolis Tower to participate in online ink battles.

Inkopolis Tower is the gathering spot for all ink battle participants. Come here if you want to compete in online Turf Wars or ranked Splat Zones matches. Upon choosing a game mode, you enter a matchmaking screen where you're grouped with seven other players—three teammates and four opponents. Competing in ink battles earns you Battle Points (or BP), which are then converted into gold. You can use gold earned from online matches to purchase new weapons and gear from the shops at Booyah Base. For more information on how online matches work, flip ahead to the Ink Battles chapter.

Fellow Inklings

You can interact with other Inklings in the Plaza—these characters belong to other players. Simply approach an Inkling and press the A button. Here you can review an Inkling's level and rank as well as their equipped weapons and gear. If you're level four or higher and see a piece of gear you like, you can order it from Spyke.

Booyah Base

Spend your hard-earned gold on new weapons, clothing, shoes, and headgear at the shops in Booyah Base.

Booyah Base consists of four shops where you can purchase new weapons and gear for use during ink battles. But you'll need to earn some street cred before shopping here—The armor vendors won't sell you stuff until you're Level 4, however Sheldon (Ammo Knights) will start selling you weapons at Level 2. So head to Inkopolis Tower and start making a name for yourself (and earning gold) by competing in ink battles. For more information on the shops and their inventory, reference the Weapons and Gear chapter.

Note

The higher your level, the more likely you are to find rare (three star) items in the gear shops. Rare items have three sub ability slots, granting your Inkling more performance-enhancing attributes.

Jelly Fresh

Tired of that boring, old Basic Tee? Then pay Jelonzo a visit at Jelly Fresh. Here you can find a variety of t-shirts, jackets, and tops, perfect for your next ink battle. Jelonzo's inventory is limited to six items per day. But stock is updated daily, so check back frequently.

Shrimp Kicks

Crusty Sean is the proprietor of Shrimp Kicks, the Plaza's exclusive source for the latest and greatest fashions in footwear. The store's stock is rotated daily, offering six different pairs of shoes per day. So stop by often to see what Crusty Sean has in stock.

Cooler Heads

If you're looking for a new hat, headband, or eyewear, then check in with Annie at Cooler Heads— the clownfish living in her anemone hairdo is Moe. Like the other gear shops, you can find six different items for sale here each day. Make daily visits to find that perfect head accessory.

Ammo Knights

Sheldon, the talkative shopkeeper of Ammo Knights, sells and manufactures a variety of weapons designed for ink battles. Unlike the other shops, the number of weapons available for purchase increases based on your level— the higher your level, the more weapons are unlocked. Sheldon can also create new weapons by using blueprints. Blueprints are obtained from the Sunken Scrolls retrieved after boss battles during the single-player campaign.

Miiverse

Interact with this orange box in the Plaza to make a post to Miiverse. While hanging out in the Plaza, your post will appear above your Inkling's head, visible by other players. In addition, your Miiverse posts can show up in other player's games as graffiti around the Plaza and on stages during ink battles.

9

Octo Valley

Cap'n Cuttlefish knows who is behind the disappearance of the Great Zapfish. Enter this hatch to investigate.

Who is that peeking out of the hatch? Why it's none other than Cap'n Cuttlefish, a decorated veteran of the Great Turf War. The disappearance of the Great Zapfish has Cap'n Cuttlefish concerned—he believes the Octarians are involved. While most Inklings ignore Cap'n Cuttlefish's seemingly paranoid ramblings, he might be on to something. Enter this hatch to meet with Cap'n Cuttlefish, launching the game's single-player campaign. Completing the campaign gives you access to new weapons and gear you can use in ink battles. Flip ahead to the Octo Valley chapter for more details.

Inkopolis News

Stay tuned to Inkopolis News for the latest announcements from Callie and Marie. They offer updates on the latest happenings in Inkopolis, including summaries of the current ink battle stages. Stay Fresh!

Battle Dojo

The Battle Dojo, located on the Plaza's upper promenade, allows you to participate in a one-on-one Balloon Battle with a friend. This isn't an online mode, but a local battle where one player plays on the TV and the other plays on the GamePad—the player using the TV can use the Classic Controller, Classic Controller Pro, or Wii U Pro Controller. Once a second controller has been connected, both players can select from eight

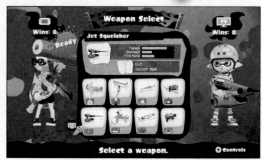

At the Battle Dojo, choose your weapon, then go head-to-head against a friend in a Balloon Battle match.

weapons, each with their own sub weapon—this is a good opportunity to try out different weapons and sub weapons before you buy them. After weapon selection, choose from one of five stages to fight over, including the same arenas available during ink battles—this is a great way to get familiar with each stage before competing online.

Battle Dojo Weapon Line-up

Weapon	Name	Sub Weapon	Name
	Splattershot		Burst Bomb
	Splat Roller		Suction Bomb
	Splat Charger		Splat Bomb
	Blaster		Disruptor
	Jet Squelcher		Splash Wall
	Aerospray MG		Seeker
	Classic Squiffer		Point Sensor
	Rapid Blaster		Ink Mine

Battle Dojo Specials

During Balloon Battle matches, look for these Canned Specials hidden in orange crates. Touching these items automatically activates a randomized special, like Inkstrike, Inkzooka, or Bubbler. Collect as many of these Canned Specials as possible to gain an edge over your opponent.

Balloon Battle

If you have the lead, keep your distance from your opponent—if you get splatted, you'll lose balloon points.

Balloon Battle is a completely unique game mode to the Battle Dojo. The objective of Balloon Battle is simple—pop more balloons than your opponent. Each balloon you pop gives you one balloon point. If you accrue thirty balloon points, you win. Otherwise, the player with the most balloon points at the end of the five-minute match wins. However, there are a couple of twists.

In the last minute of gameplay, each balloon you pop is worth two balloon points, making the final moments of a match much more intense. Also, if you get splatted by an opponent, you'll lose balloon points. So if your opponent has a commanding lead, instead of going after balloons, try to splat them in an attempt to even the scores. There are no rewards issued for competing in Balloon Battles, but the experience you gain here can make all the difference once you transition to online battles.

Note

During Balloon Battles, these spiral indicators show where a new batch of balloons is about to appear. Get to this area before your opponent in an attempt to pop all the new balloons. But be careful—your opponent might be hiding nearby with the same idea.

Arcade Games

The arcade cabinet in the Plaza features a mini-game you can play called Squid Jump. This, and all arcade games, are played on the GamePad. Look down at the GamePad's screen to help your squid navigate a series of platforms. By default, Squid Jump is the only arcade game available. But you can unlock more by defeating the Octobot King with the Inkling Boy, Inkling Girl, and Inkling Squid amiibo. In addition to playing arcade games at the cabinet in the Plaza, you can also play these games while waiting in the lobby of Inkopolis Tower—play a few rounds while waiting for other players to join your game.

Interact with this arcade cabinet to play a game of Squid Jump—other games can be unlocked by completing amiibo challenges.

Squid Jump

Unlock: Default

Squid Jump puts you in control of a squid who must leap vertically from one platform to the next. There are a total of twenty-five stages to complete. Gather the red fish, blue fish, and the red starfish to enhance your jumping ability.

Squidball

Unlock: Defeat the Octobot King as Inkling Girl amiibo

Squidball is a volleyball-style game requiring you to knock back an Zapfish at your jellyfish opponents—use the left stick to aim the Zapfish at the jellyfish targets. Eliminate the required number of jellyfish to advance to the next stage.

Squid Racer

Unlock: Defeat the Octobot King as Inkling Boy amiibo

Squid Racer pits your squid against jellyfish in a road race. Hold down the ZL Button to drift around corners, then accelerate out of the turn at the right moment to gain a sudden burst of speed. Keep an eye on the timer and complete each stage before time expires.

Squid Beatz

Unlock: Defeat the Octobot King as Inkling Squid amiibo

Squid Beatz features the different music found throughout *Splatoon*. You can simply listen to the music or participate in a mini-game on the GamePad. There are no points or stages in this game, just some simple rhythm-based interactivity.

Judd

If you earn a vibe rank of Toasty, Smokin', or SO HAWT!!, Judd will reward you with gold.

When he's not officiating ink battles, Judd can be found snoozing on this blue box in the Plaza. Speak to Judd to get tips for your upcoming ink battles. But Judd serves another purpose too. By winning ink battles, you increase your vibe rank, visible in the Inkopolis Tower lobby screen. There are four vibe ranks: Chill, Toasty, Smokin', and SO HAWT!! If you obtain a rank of Toasty or higher, Judd will give you a daily gold reward—the higher the rank, the more gold you'll receive. So make a habit of talking to Judd each day, preferably at the end of your play session. Vibe ranks reset every day, so if you forget to talk to Judd, you're leaving gold behind. For more information on Judd and vibe ranks, reference the Ink Battles chapter.

Spyke

Sitting in the alley, opposite of Booyah Base, Spyke is running a different type of business. But like the more legitimate shop owners, Spyke won't deal with you until you reach level four or higher. At that point you can place orders with Spyke by interacting with other Inklings in the Plaza. If you see an Inkling wearing clothing, shoes, or headgear you like, place an order with Spyke—he'll have the item you want the next day. You can place up to three orders at a time, but Spyke will only deliver one item per day, in the order in which they were requested. You can also pay Spyke Super Sea Snails (obtained from Splatfests) to reroll the sub abilities assigned to your clothing, shoes, or headgear. For more information on Spyke (and Splatfest), flip ahead to the Ink Battles chapter.

Need some gear not offered in the other shops? Spyke can help you out.

amiibo SUPPORT

Place one of the three Splatoon amiibo figures on the GamePad to access new challenges and rewards.

Three new amiibo figures have been created to coincide with the release of *Splatoon*: Inkling Girl, Inkling Boy, and Inkling Squid. Interact with the empty amiibo box in the Plaza. Here you're prompted to place one of the three amiibo figures on the GamePad—the corresponding amiibo appears within the box on screen. Each amiibo figure unlocks a variety of content including rewards like gold, weapons, gear, and arcade mini-games. But in order to earn these rewards, you must first complete specific challenges.

Note

Only the three *Splatoon* amiibo figures are compatible with the game. But the *Splatoon* figures can be used to unlock content in *Hyrule Warriors*, *Mario Party 10*, and *Captain Toad: Treasure Tracker*.

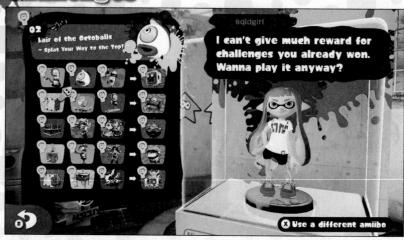

Even if you've completed all the stages and boss fights in the single-player campaign, playing them again as each amiibo presents unique challenges and some cool rewards.

After placing an amiibo figure on the GamePad, that amiibo is unlocked in the game and can take part in a variety of challenges. The challenges consist of three stages and one Boss per zone, taken from the single-player campaign. Completing these stages earns you gold—see the provided table for reward breakdowns per stage. Defeating bosses unlocks other rewards, like unique weapons, clothing, shoes, headgear, and arcade mini-games. You must complete these stages and boss fights while playing as your character. But instead of using the standard-issue Hero Shot and single-player sub weapons, you must use the weapons associated with the unlocked amiibo. For example, the Inkling Boy must complete the stages and boss fights while using a roller weapon. This adds some variety to the single-player stages and boss fights, forcing you to approach them in a different way. See the following listings of each amiibo for details on how to unlock every reward.

Challenges: Gold Rewards

Stage	Gold
Challenge 1 (Zone 1)	600
Challenge 2 (Zone 1)	700
Challenge 3 (Zone 1)	800
Challenge 4 (Zone 2)	900
Challenge 5 (Zone 2)	1,000
Challenge 6 (Zone 2)	1,100
Challenge 7 (Zone 3)	1,200
Challenge 8 (Zone 3)	1,300
Challenge 9 (Zone 3)	1,400
Challenge 10 (Zone 4)	1,500
Challenge 11 (Zone 4)	1,600
Challenge 12 (Zone 4)	1,700
Challenge 13 (Zone 5)	1,800
Challenge 14 (Zone 5)	1,900
Challenge 15 (Zone 5)	2,000

Note

You can replay the challenges after you've completed them, but you'll only receive a reward of 100 gold for each subsequent completion.

Inkling Girl

RELEASE DATE: May 29, 2015

DESCRIPTION: Inkling girls hail from the city of Inkopolis in the game *Splatoon*. They crave team-based competition and love to customize their gear before participating in the hottest sport in town, Turf War! Their hobbies include making messes, rocking the latest fashions, dancing, and spoiling the nefarious plans of their evil octopus archrivals, the Octarians! For realsies!

Weapon Unlock: Hero Charger Replica

SUB WEAPON: SPLAT BOMB

SPECIAL: BOMB RUSH

Unlock Criteria: Obtain the weapon blueprint by defeating the Octomaw.

Arcade Game: Squidball

Unlock Criteria: Defeat the Octobot King.

Gear Rewards

Gear	Name	Rarity	Main Ability	Criteria
	Squid Hairclip	★★	Swim Speed Up	Defeat the Octostomp
	School Uniform	★★	Ink Recovery Up	Defeat the Octonozzle
	School Shoes	★★	Ink Saver (Sub)	Defeat the Octowhirl

Challenge Notes

The Inkling Girl is equipped with a charger weapon, requiring you to hold down the ZR button to completely charge it. The aiming reticle is surrounded by a ring-shaped gauge, showing the status of the weapon's charge. When fully charged, the weapon emits a narrow, high-pressure stream of ink, ideal for long-range engagements. The weapon is less effective at spreading ink, so utilize multiple low-charge shots to spread ink around your feet while moving and swimming through stages.

Inkling Boy

RELEASE DATE: May 29, 2015

DESCRIPTION: Inkling boys hail from the city of Inkopolis in the game *Splatoon*. They crave team-based competition and love to customize their gear before participating in the hottest sport in town, Turf War! Their hobbies include making messes, rocking the latest fashions, dancing, and spoiling the nefarious plans of their evil octopus archrivals, the Octarians! Like a boss!

Weapon Unlock: Hero Roller Replica

SUB WEAPON: SUCTION BOMB

SPECIAL: KILLER WAIL

Unlock Criteria: Obtain the weapon blueprint by defeating the Octomaw.

Arcade Game: Squid Racer

Unlock Criteria: Defeat the Octobot King.

Gear Rewards

Gear	Name	Rarity	Main Ability	Criteria
	Samurai Helmet	★★	Damage Up	Defeat the Octostomp
	Samurai Jacket	★★	Special Charge Up	Defeat the Octonozzle
	Samurai Shoes	★★	Special Duration Up	Defeat the Octowhirl

Challenge Notes

When playing as the Inkling Boy, you're equipped with a roller. This is a highly versatile weapon, but it takes some getting used to. While rolling across horizontal surfaces, the roller is great for spreading ink and rolling right over enemies. When it comes to spreading ink on vertical surfaces or hitting enemies above or below you, swing the roller to splat ink over a wide area. Or at close range, a well-timed swing can result in a lethal melee strike—hide in your ink, then jump out to whack enemies before they can retaliate.

Inkling Squid

RELEASE DATE: May 29, 2015

DESCRIPTION: In the game *Splatoon*, the main characters, Inklings, can instantly transform into squids! We're not sure what marvel of anatomy allows them to perform this majestic feat, but it sure is sweet. In squid form, Inklings can swim in any surface they've splattered with ink, even up walls! They can also hide from opponents by submerging in ink and keeping still. How cool is that?

Weapon Unlock: Hero Shot Replica

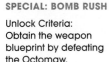

SUB WEAPON: BURST BOMB

SPECIAL: BOMB RUSH

Unlock Criteria: Obtain the weapon blueprint by defeating the Octomaw.

Arcade Game: Squid Beatz

Unlock Criteria: Defeat the Octobot King.

Gear Rewards

Gear	Name	Rarity	Main Ability	Criteria
	Power Mask	★★	Defense Up	Defeat the Octostomp
	Power Armor	★★	Quick Respawn	Defeat the Octonozzle
	Power Boots	★★	Ink Saver (Main)	Defeat the Octowhirl

Challenge Notes

The Inkling Squid is perhaps the most powerful *Splatoon* amiibo. By default, you play as a regular Inkling. But instead of turning into a squid when holding down the ZL button, you transform into an invincible Kraken. This is just like playing the Kraken special in ink battles. If the Kraken seems overpowered, it's because you're tasked with clearing each stage within a specific amount of time or with limited ink. When playing a challenge with limited ink, avoid using sub weapons to keep your ink tank from being depleted.

Note

The Inkling Squid amiibo figure is available exclusively in the *Splatoon* series three-pack set.

OCTO VALLEY

INTRODUCTION

Upon your arrival in Octo Valley, you're immediately greeted by Cap'n Cuttlefish, leader of the Squidbeak Splatoon. He theorizes that the Great Zapfish, missing from Inkopolis Tower, has been stolen by the Octarians as revenge for their defeat in the Great Turf War 100 years ago—though nobody else believes him. He needs your help to rescue the Great Zapfish, assigning you as Agent 3 of the New Squidbeak Splatoon. He even gives you a Hero Suit—handed down from Agents 1 and 2. Do you have what it takes to rescue the Great Zapfish? Or has Cap'n Cuttlefish completely overestimated your capabilities? Fortunately, this chapter has all the information you need to overcome each obstacle and outwit every Octarian you encounter during your search for the Great Zapfish.

Interface

Respawn Meter

Sunken Scroll Status

Power Eggs

Special Gauge

Aiming Reticle

Sub Weapons

Aiming Reticle

This white ring icon in the center of the screen is your weapon's reticle. Place it over a target and fire to spread ink.

Respawn Meter

Think of these three bars as lives. They represent how many times you can respawn after getting splatted or falling off a stage—you lose one bar after each splat. However, one bar is replenished with each new checkpoint you cross.

Sunken Scroll Status

This icon indicates whether you've located a stage's Sunken Scroll or not. If the icon is grayed out, you still need to find it.

Power Eggs

This counter displays how many Power Eggs you've collected. Use Power Eggs to purchase upgrades for your weapons and gear.

Special Gauge

This gauge appears when you've obtained an Inkzooka, Bubbler, or Bomb Rush special. Each special can be activated for a limited time. The gauge rapidly empties while a special is active, indicating how much time is left.

Sub Weapons

These three icons represent your equipped sub weapons, including Splat Bombs, Burst Bombs, and Seekers. Use the +Control Pad to select the active sub weapon.

Octarian Lairs

■ *Splat the invisible lair entrances with ink to reveal them.*

There are a total of twenty-seven hidden Octarian lair entrances scattered throughout Octo Valley, not including the five Boss Kettles.

These lairs are divided amongst five different zones. Infiltrate and complete each lair in a zone to unlock a boss kettle, allowing you to fight each zone's boss. Once a boss is defeated, you can proceed to the next zone. But before you can enter a lair, you must first find it. Lairs are cloaked, invisible to the naked eye. However, if you repeatedly splat a lair entrance with ink, it becomes visible, allowing you to enter. Each revealed lair appears on the GamePad's map. By tapping the lair icons on this map, you can Super Jump from one lair to another for easy access.

Power Eggs and Upgrades

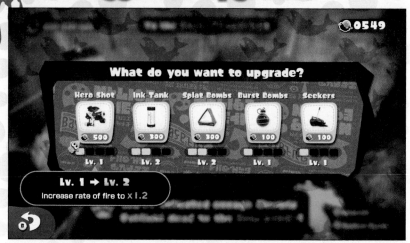

What do you want to upgrade?

🎮 0549

Hero Shot	Ink Tank	Splat Bombs	Burst Bombs	Seekers
500	300	300	100	100
Lv. 1	Lv. 2	Lv. 2	Lv. 1	Lv. 1

Lv. 1 ➜ Lv. 2
Increase rate of fire to ✕ 1.2

■ *What are you saving all those Power Eggs for? Buy some upgrades!*

While advancing through the various Octarian lairs, you'll collect Power Eggs. Power Eggs are earned by defeating enemies, but can also be retrieved from lairs by simply touching them or splatting them with ink. Power Eggs function like currency, allowing you to purchase upgrades for your existing gear as well as purchase new weapons. Initially you come equipped with a Hero Shot, ink tank, and Splat Bombs—all three can be upgraded to enhance their performance. Or you can purchase Burst Bombs and Seekers, sub weapons that can also be upgraded. So before entering a new lair, review how many Power Eggs you have and consider purchasing some upgrades. There's no other use for Power Eggs, so you might as well spend them.

Research Notes

■ *Reference the lair maps in this chapter to locate every Sunken Scroll.*

Each lair (and boss) holds one Sunken Scroll. These collectibles are usually hidden, tucked away within orange crates. Once retrieved, they're automatically revealed after completing a lair or boss fight. These scrolls contain pieces of backstory, giving you more insight on life in Inkopolis as well as historical details pertaining to the conflicts between Inklings and the Octarians. While in Octo Valley, you can review the contents of your collected Sunken Scrolls at any time by accessing your research notes. Sunken Scrolls recovered from bosses allow Sheldon, at Ammo Knights, to create new weapons for use in ink battles.

EQUIPMENT

Fortunately, you're not going into battle empty handed. You've been outfitted with some of the finest gear Cap'n Cuttlefish has to offer, including the Hero Shot. You can also find armor and specials hidden in crates during your journeys through each Octarian lair. So smash every orange crate you see—you never know what you might find inside.

Weapons and Upgrades

Hero Shot

Upgrades

Level	Description	Cost
1	Default	—
2	Increase Rate of Fire to x1.2	500
3	Increase Rate of Fire to x1.5	1,000
4	Increase Rate of Fire to x2.0	1,500

The Hero Shot is your primary weapon throughout your fight against the Octarians, ideal for inking territory and splatting opponents. You can spend power eggs to increase the weapon's rate of fire. Initially, these upgrades are quite expensive—your power eggs are probably better spent on increasing your ink tank's capacity or unlocking Burst Bombs or Seekers. But as you progress deeper into Octo Valley, the increased rate of fire comes in handy when confronting bosses and tough enemies like Octolings, Octobombers, and Octostrikers. Keep in mind, an increased rate of fire will make the weapon consume more ink, so consider upgrading your ink tank's capacity to compensate.

Ink Tank

Upgrades

Level	Description	Cost
1	Default	—
2	Increase tank capacity to x1.2	100
3	Increase tank capacity to x1.5	300
4	Increase tank capacity to x2.0	800

Worn on your Inkling's back, this ink tank supplies ink for your Hero Shot and sub weapons. The more you deploy your weapons, the more ink is consumed. The ink tank slowly refills over time, but you can increase the replenishment rate by diving into your ink in squid form. The arrow icon on the side of the tank indicates how much ink your selected sub weapon will consume—take this into account before tossing a Splat Bomb, Burst Bomb, or Seeker. Upgrading the ink tank increases its capacity. This is a very worthwhile upgrade, so don't hesitate in maxing it out. The greater the tank's ink capacity, the longer you can use your weapon without running out of ink.

Splat Bombs

Upgrades

Level	Description	Cost
1	Default	—
2	Increase blast area to x1.3	100
3	Increase blast area to x1.6	300
4	Increase blast area to x1.8	800

Splat Bombs are your default sub weapon and can be thrown to spread ink or splat enemies. Think of these like grenades. Hold down the R button to view and adjust the bomb's arc-like trajectory. When you're satisfied with the bomb's flight path, release the R button to throw it. Splat Bombs utilize a delayed fuse, allowing them to bounce off walls or skip across the ground before exploding. This makes them great for engaging enemies indirectly while hiding behind cover. Initially Splat Bombs have a modest, but effective, blast radius. The blast radius can be expanded by upgrading the weapon. Of all the sub weapon upgrades, the Splat Bomb upgrades are the most worthwhile.

Burst Bombs

Upgrades

Level	Description	Cost
1	Unlock Weapon	100
2	Increase blast area to x1.3	100
3	Increase blast area to x1.6	300
4	Increase blast area to x1.8	800

Burst Bombs must be purchased before they're added to your arsenal, costing only 100 Power Eggs. In terms of deployment, these hand-tossed sub weapons function identically to the Splat Bombs. However, instead of utilizing a delayed fuse, Burst Bombs explode as soon as they touch the ground or foes. These bombs also have a noticeably smaller blast radius than Splat Bombs, so you'll need to score direct hits with these bombs if you hope to splat an enemy. This makes Burst Bombs a bit more challenging to deploy offensively. Instead, use them primarily to spread ink, particularly along vertical surfaces. Once unlocked, upgrading this weapon shouldn't be a priority.

Seekers

Upgrades

Level	Description	Cost
1	Unlock Weapon	100
2	Increase blast area to x1.3	100
3	Increase blast area to x1.6	300
4	Increase blast area to x1.8	800

Like Burst Bombs, Seekers must be purchased before they're unlocked. These unique weapons are bombs that cruise along the ground, homing in on foes. When an enemy is in sight, hold down the R button to target them with a Seeker, then release the R button to launch the weapon. The Seeker will try to hit the enemy, even if the enemy moves. Beyond their homing ability, Seekers are most useful for spreading ink. When traveling along the ground, Seekers leave behind a narrow trail of ink. Swim through this ink trail to stealthily move deep into enemy territory without being spotted. In addition to increasing the Seerker's blast radius, the upgrades also increase the width of its ink trail. This can come in handy if you like swimming behind your Seekers.

Armor and Specials

Armor

Next to Power Eggs, armor is the second-most common pick-up you're likely to find in orange crates. Simply make contact with this briefcase-like object to equip armor. Not only does this change the appearance of your Inkling, but it also allows you to take more damage without getting splatted. If you take heavy damage while wearing armor, the armor is destroyed, breaking to pieces—but it's better than getting splatted. You can equip up to three pieces of armor at a time—the second and third pieces are represented by antenna protruding from your Inkling's helmet.

Inkzooka

Yes, this special is like a bazooka that fires ink. Once activated, you can fire the Inkzooka repeatedly for approximately five seconds. Each shot consists of a tall tornado of ink, zooming across the stage. Inkzookas are great for taking out enemies, but they also leave behind a thin trail of ink. When fired at a vertical surface, it leaves a trail behind you can swim up in squid form. But watch your footing when firing this weapon—each shot knocks you back. If you're not careful, the recoil could knock you off a ledge or push you back into a puddle of enemy ink.

Bubbler

The Bubbler special generates an impenetrable bubble around your Inkling, making them invincible for short period of time. This special is best deployed when you are confronted by multiple enemies. Although you can't take damage while the Bubbler is active, you can still get knocked around by heavy attacks. Splat Bombs tossed by Octobombers and Octolings can push you around, potentially knocking you off ledges. Although durable, the Bubbler can't save you from plummeting off the side of a stage. So do your best to avoid explosive attacks.

Bomb Rush

Bomb Rush gives you the ability to throw an unlimited number of Splat Bombs, Burst Bombs, or Seekers for a short period of time. While Bomb Rush is active, these sub weapons consume no ink, so don't let this opportunity go to waste. If you want to spread ink over vast distances, use Seekers to send trails of ink in all directions. Or if you're on the attack, use Splat Bombs to overwhelm Octotroopers and other enemies in your path.

Note

Armor is always active, but you must activate specials like Inkzooka, Bubbler, and Bomb Rush. Click down on the Right Control Stick to activate specials. You can only carry one special at a time. Picking up a new special will replace the one currently equipped, so make a habit of using a special before grabbing a new one.

OCTO VALLEY FEATURES

Your journey through Octo Valley takes you to some interesting (and treacherous) locales. Before setting off to find the Great Zapfish, take some time to become familiar with some of the key features you'll interact with during your adventure.

Lair Entrance

Before you can enter an Octarian lair, you must first locate and reveal its entrance. These invisible entrances are scattered across each zone. Splat them repeatedly with ink until they become visible, then stand on top of them and press the ZL button to enter the lair.

Power Eggs

Power Eggs are the currency in Octo Valley, allowing you to purchase upgrades for your weapons and equipment. These are often found in orange crates and balloons, but can also be found scattered across Octarian lairs. You can collect Power Eggs by touching them or splatting them with ink. So if a Power Egg appears to be out of reach, try to find a way to hit it with ink.

Crates

Crates are found in every Octarian lair, but pay special attention to orange crates—these contain Power Eggs, Sunken Scrolls, armor, or specials. Simply shoot crates to smash them, then grab whatever is inside. Before destroying a crate, make sure you don't need to use it for concealment—they're handy for hiding behind.

Balloons

These orange balloons are a common sight throughout Octo Valley. Splat them with ink to make them pop. Balloons are always filled with Power Eggs. Popping a balloon automatically retrieves all the Power Eggs inside it.

Launchpads

Most Octarian lairs consist of multiple platforms. Launchpads are used to access distant platforms. Simply stand on a launchpad and press the ZL button to perform a Super Jump to the next platform. But before using a launchpad, make sure you've thoroughly explored the current platform. Launchpads are a one-way trip—there's no way to jump back.

Checkpoints

Walk across checkpoints to save your progress while advancing through Octarian lairs. You'll usually hit these checkpoints automatically after using a launchpad. In the event that you're splatted or fall off a ledge, you'll resume your progress from the most recent checkpoint. Each checkpoint you activate gives you one more life.

Sunken Scrolls

There is one Sunken Scroll hidden within each Octarian lair, usually contained within an orange crate. But they can also be retrieved at the end of boss battles. These scrolls reveal a variety of story information and are collected in your research notes. Sunken Scrolls retrieved from bosses contain blueprints Sheldon can use to manufacture new weapons for ink battles.

Zapfish

Before you can fight the boss of each zone, you must first collect a certain number of Zapfish. There is one Zapfish located at the end of every lair. Each Zapfish is protected by a barrier. Repeatedly shoot the barrier until it pops, then grab the Zapfish to complete the level.

Balloon Fish

These large, white balloons are found attached to vertical and horizontal surfaces. When targeted with your ink, these balloons expand before exploding, spreading your ink over a massive area. Target Balloon Fish when confronting multiple enemies—if you time it just right, one exploding Balloon Fish can take them all out. Balloon Fish are also an excellent way to spread ink, allowing you to rapidly swim across the freshly inked surfaces.

Keys and Vaults

Some Octarian lairs feature vaults that must be opened with a key. Keys are usually hidden within orange crates, but can sometimes be carried by enemies. Once you've found a key, use it to unlock a vault—simply touch the vault to open it. Vaults usually cover launchpads and other key features required to progress through a lair.

Boss Kettle

When you've collected the requisite number of Zapfish, the zone's Boss Kettle opens up, allowing you to fight a boss. These purple kettles are usually located near the center of a zone and remain closed. But once opened, step on top and press the ZL button to begin a boss battle.

Area Gate

Each zone is blocked by one of these area gates. These gates prevent you from accessing neighboring zones. However, once a zone's boss has been defeated, the area gate is destroyed. Beyond the area gate you can find a path leading to the next zone.

Gusher

When targeted with your ink, these valves burst open, emitting a tall geyser of ink. Stand on top of a Gusher before shooting it to ride the geyser like an elevator. Or if you prefer, you can swim up an active Gusher to reach the top. Gushers give you access to high platforms and other areas that would otherwise be impossible to reach. The geyser of ink can also serve as a solid pillar to hide behind—active Gushers block all incoming enemy ink.

Sponge

As these small yellow, cube-shaped sponges absorb your ink, they expand, becoming huge blocks you can swim or walk across. However, when hit with enemy ink, sponges shrink in size. If you're on top of a sponge when it shrinks, you could potentially fall—stay near the center of a sponge to mitigate the chances of falling off. Cross sponges quickly when possible and deal with threats before they can shrink the sponge beneath your feet.

Propeller Lift

Propeller Lifts are small platforms capable of horizontal or vertical movement. To activate a Propeller Lift, hop aboard and target the green propeller. Continually shoot the propeller to make the platform travel in its predetermined direction. If you stop shooting the propeller, the platform will slowly return to its original location. While moving along a Propeller Lift, you become a much harder target for enemies to hit.

Spreader

These large arm-like devices are used to spread enemy ink over large horizontal and vertical surfaces. Instead of trying to avoid the ink spread by these devices, simply advance across the Spreader itself. The top of a Spreader can be coated in your ink, allowing you to swim across the top of it.

Ink Cannon

Step behind the controls of one of these turrets and fire ink-filled missiles at distant opponents and surfaces. Upon impact, these missiles explode, spreading your ink over a wide area. But the missiles travel slowly and have a tendency to lose altitude over distance. So when engaging targets at long range, aim high to compensate for the missile's drop.

Inkrail

Target these nodes with your ink to create an Inkrail. Like launchpads, Inkrails are often used to access distant platforms. Once an Inkrail has been activated, approach it and press the ZL button to swim along it. Inkrails allow you to travel at high speeds. While speeding along an Inkrail, jump to launch your squid high into the air. But watch out for incoming enemy ink—if you're hit while traversing an Inkrail, you'll fall.

Splat Switch

Spread ink across these panels to trigger the transformation of a platform. If you can't find where to go next, look for a splat switch. Chances are you'll need to activate one of these switches to alter the platform in a way that allows you to access new areas. Once a transformation has been completed, it cannot be undone.

Pinwheel

These windmill-like devices are attached to both vertical and horizontal surfaces, making advances a bit tricky. Two of the pinwheel's arms are made out of boxy pieces of metal while the other two arms consist of nets. These arms are designed to knock you off platforms. For best results, ride along the tops of the metal arms. Otherwise, you must swim through the netted arms while jumping over the metal arms.

THE OCTARIANS

The Octarians went to great lengths to infiltrate Inkopolis and steal the Great Zapfish, so you can bet they're not going to return it without putting up a fight. You'll encounter a variety of enemies during your adventures in Octo Valley, each with their strengths and weaknesses. Here are some pointers for surviving each hostile encounter.

Octotrooper

Octotroopers are the foot soldiers of the Octarians and the most common enemy you'll encounter. They come in two variants: fixed and moving. The fixed Octotrooper remains in a stationary position, manning a slow-firing turret. The moving Octotroopers patrol through purple ink, also manning a slow-firing turret. Whether fixed or moving, Octotroopers don't pose a huge threat. Spread ink near them and try to sneak up on them, splatting them at close range with your Hero Shot. Or toss a Splat Bomb in their direction—if they can, they'll try to get away, sometimes running off the side of a platform.

Twintacle Octotrooper

Recognizable by their two tentacles, Twintacle Octotroopers perform just like standard Octotroopers. However, they're equipped with faster firing turrets, making them a much more formidable threat. While you can easily dodge the incoming blobs of ink fired by Octotroopers, these more-advanced enemies fire narrow, fast-moving streams of purple ink. Avoid face-to-face encounters when possible. Instead, swim through your ink and take them by surprise, shooting them in the back with your Hero Shot. Or simply stay behind cover and take them out with Splat Bombs.

Shielded Octotrooper

Like the standard Octotroopers and Twintacle Octotroopers, these shielded enemies come in fixed and moving variants. But what sets them apart is the metal shield attached to the front of their turret. Unless using an Inkzooka, you can't shoot through or destroy this shield, so you must find a way to flank them. Try spreading ink around them and sneaking up on them from behind. Or toss a Splat Bomb behind them—the Octotrooper will rotate to face the Splat Bomb, leaving their back exposed. Whatever you do, don't stand in front of one of these enemies and exchange ink—you won't win this duel.

Octopod

They may look cute, but Octopods have nothing but bad intentions. These enemies come running at you at high speed. If they get close, they'll explode, spreading purple ink over a wide area, potentially splatting you. To avoid such attacks, lay a line of ink between you and the approaching Octopods. Your ink will slow down their advance considerably, allowing you to pick them off one by one. Octopods usually attack in groups, so make sure you have plenty of ink spread out to ensnare all attackers.

Octoball

Octoballs roll across horizontal surfaces, spreading wide trails of purple ink behind them. If you're detected, they'll come rolling straight at you dealing heavy damage upon contact. As with the Octopods, your first goal with Octoballs is to slow them down. Spread a wide line of your ink in an approaching Octoball's path. As they come into contact with your ink, their speed is slowed immensely. But they won't stop inching their way toward you. Before they get too close, repeatedly shoot the Octoball until it explodes, spreading your ink over a wide area. Seekers are also effective against these enemies.

Squee-G

Unlike most enemies, Squee-Gs don't pose a direct threat. Instead, they simply mop up ink. They usually patrol walls and other vertical surfaces, quickly responding to any ink you spread. Squee-Gs can't be destroyed, so you must simply avoid them. Ink a wall and swim past them before they can clean up your ink. They're not particularly fast, so as long as you swim past them quickly, you shouldn't have many problems with these little guys.

Octobomber

These large enemies hover in mid air while tossing Splat Bombs. Since they make no contact with the ground, Splat Bombs and Seekers are usually ineffective when targeting these enemies directly. Instead, try to sneak up on Octobombers without being seen and splat them at close range with your Hero Shot. While hiding behind cover, toss Splat Bombs or Burst Bombs in an attempt to ink the area around an Octobomber. When the surface below an Octobomber is inked, swim forward and attack.

Octocopter

Like Octobombers, Octocopters are airborne threats. But instead of attacking with Splat Bombs, they fire slow-moving blobs of purple ink—much like the Octotroopers. For best results, stay hidden until you can pop up out of your ink and ambush Octocopters with your Hero Shot at close range. While you can't hit Octocopters with a Seeker, swimming within a Seeker's ink trail is a great way to sneak up on these guys.

Octostamp

If you're detected by an Octostamp, they'll come running at you before leaping into the air—this is your cue to move out of the way. Don't try shooting them while they're running at you, as hitting them in the face won't do any damage. Instead, wait until they land face down on a platform, then shoot them in their exposed back. Alternatively, coax them to an edge of a platform and side step as they inadvertently leap off the edge.

Octoling

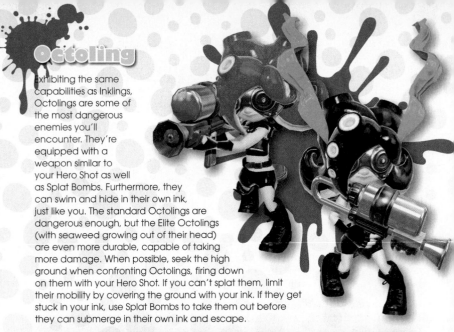

Exhibiting the same capabilities as Inklings, Octolings are some of the most dangerous enemies you'll encounter. They're equipped with a weapon similar to your Hero Shot as well as Splat Bombs. Furthermore, they can swim and hide in their own ink, just like you. The standard Octolings are dangerous enough, but the Elite Octolings (with seaweed growing out of their head) are even more durable, capable of taking more damage. When possible, seek the high ground when confronting Octolings, firing down on them with your Hero Shot. If you can't splat them, limit their mobility by covering the ground with your ink. If they get stuck in your ink, use Splat Bombs to take them out before they can submerge in their own ink and escape.

Tip

If you want to practice for ink battles, repeat the lairs occupied by Octolings. Fights against these enemies closely match the action you'll face in online battles. Also, many of these stages are repurposed in ink battles, allowing you to get familiar with each arena.

Octostriker

You'll encounter a total of four Octostrikers during your adventure. These enemies hover above flying saucers at the end of each stage while targeting you with Inkstrikes. These attacks consist of massive ink tornados. To avoid getting targeted with an Inkstrike, stay on the move, swimming through your ink when possible to prevent detection. When you reach the flying saucer, aggressively pursue the Octostriker around the perimeter—ink the surface and swim up to him, hitting him repeatedly with your Hero Shot until he explodes. Speed and mobility are key when confronting these enemies.

Octodiver

If you see large swaths of purple ink, there's a good chance an Octodiver is hiding beneath the surface, waiting to ambush you. These enemies perform just like their Octotrooper and Twintacle Octotrooper counterparts, but have the ability to stay submerged within their ink until they encounter a threat. To avoid getting taken by surprise, take time to spread ink whenever you encounter large pools of purple ink. This can force Octodivers to the surface, making them easier to engage. There's even a shielded variant of the Octodiver. If a Shielded Octodiver is encountered at close range, immediately swim away to avoid getting splatted by their incoming blasts of purple ink. This may be a good opportunity to use an Inkzooka—even that shield won't block the Inkzooka's devastating shots.

Flooder

Towering above platforms on four stilt-like legs, Flooders constantly patrol, raining down purple ink. Like Squee-Gs, Flooders can't be destroyed, so you must avoid them. For best results, stay submerged in your ink to avoid being spotted. The Flooder's red targeting laser constantly scans for foes, and if you're detected, they'll move toward you. Break line of sight to avoid being chased by a Flooder. Seekers come in handy during these encounters, allowing you to spread long lines of ink you can swim through. But maintain situational awareness at all times. Otherwise multiple Flooders may converge on your location, leaving you no path of escape.

Octosniper

These long-range specialists are extremely dangerous, capable of hitting you at distances where you can't retaliate. Their turret fires a narrow steam of ink, capable of inflicting heavy damage. Watch the Octosniper's green targeting laser to determine which way the enemy is facing. When they're looking away, try to sneak up on them by spreading and swimming through your ink. Once close enough, hide behind cover and lob Splat Bombs in an Octosniper's direction. If you can't close the deal with Splat Bombs, ink an area next to the enemy, then swim through your ink, ambushing the Octosniper at close range with your Hero Shot.

ZONE 1

Welcome to your first stop in Octo Valley. Cap'n Cuttlefish is grateful for your assistance in the fight against the Octarians. But do you have what it takes to rescue the Great Zapfish and restore power to Inkopolis? There are three areas you must clear in this zone, followed by an epic battle against the first boss—the Octostomp.

Zone 1

Area Gate

BB

O2

O3

Inkopolis Plaza

O1

Legend

O1	Octotrooper Hideout	**O3**	Rise of the Octocopters
O2	Lair of the Octoballs	**BB**	Boss Battle: The Mighty Octostomp

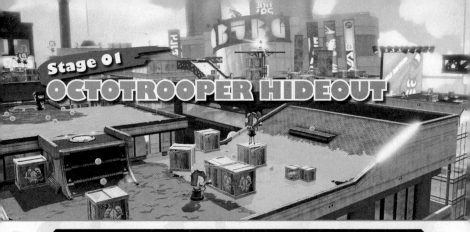

Stage 01
OCTOTROOPER HIDEOUT

Octotrooper Hideout

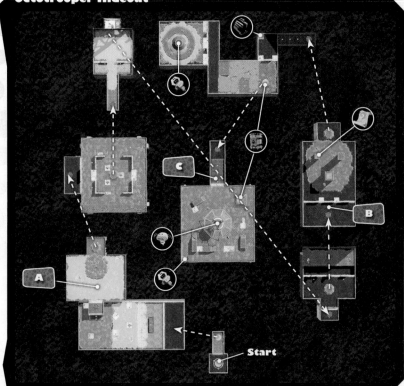

A

C

B

Start

Legend

Key Locations		Armor	
Sunken Scroll		Inkzooka	
Key		Bubbler	
Vault		Bomb Rush	
Zapfish		Jump Path	

A

The Shielded Octotrooper here is manning a turret with a protective shield. A frontal attack is not possible, as the shield always protects the Octotrooper from taking damage. Therefore, swim through the ink and flank the Octotrooper from the side. If you can't eliminate this enemy

with one attack, duck back into the your ink and swim to another flanking position on the opposite side of the platform. You can also throw Splat Bombs to distract these enemies-shoot them in their exposed back as they rotate to face the Splat Bomb.

B

There are five Octotroopers patrolling this platform. Take the fight to new heights by inking one of the pillars with your ink and swimming to the top, firing down on the Octotroopers from above. Attacking from elevated positions gives you a huge advantage— these guys won't even see you.

When you've eliminated all the enemies, don't head for the launchpad just yet— there's a Sunken Scroll nearby!

Sunken Scroll

This level's Sunken Scroll is located atop this platform's tallest pillar. Ink the side of the pillar, swim to the top, and smash the crate to retrieve the scroll.

C

There's a vault on this platform, as well as two Octotroopers, including a Shielded Octotrooper. Cut into the enemy's purple territory with your your ink, then swim to close range and ambush the Octotroopers. The key is located in one of the orange crates at the back of the platform. But after retrieving the key, watch for

three more Octotroopers appearing near the vault. Swim through your ink to sneak up on these threats and eliminate them one by one before approaching the vault. Once opened, the vault reveals a launchpad leading to the Zapfish. Shoot the yellow barrier imprisoning the Zapfish, then move in for the rescue.

Stage 02
LAIR OF THE OCTOBALLS

Lair of the Octoballs

B

A

C

Start

Legend

	Key Locations		Armor
	Sunken Scroll		Inkzooka
	Key		Bubbler
	Vault		Bomb Rush
	Zapfish		Jump Path

Beware of the four charging Octopods—if they get close, they'll explode, damaging you with enemy ink. Instead of shooting all these Octopods individually, simply target the large Balloon Fish. When the Balloon Fish explodes, it spreads your ink over a wide area, eliminating all the Octopods. Target Balloon Fish in the future to spread ink over large swaths of territory.

Watch out for Octoballs on this platform, particularly when crossing the narrow ramp—lay down a line of ink in their path to prevent them from smacking you. Octoballs are practically helpless when submerged in your ink, making them much easier to target. But once they wiggle out of your ink, they'll continue to roll around at full speed—deal with them before they can escape.

Sunken Scroll

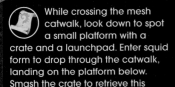

While crossing the mesh catwalk, look down to spot a small platform with a crate and a launchpad. Enter squid form to drop through the catwalk, landing on the platform below. Smash the crate to retrieve this level's Sunken Scroll, then use the launchpad to return to the catwalk.

Use the launchpad near the base of the towering wall to access this Ink Cannon. Use it to coat the distant wall with ink. While you're at it, target the floating balloons and the two Twintacle Octotroopers atop the wall. Once you've inked the entire wall, drop down to the platform below and begin swimming up the inked wall. But you must move fast—the Squee-G along the bottom portion of the wall will clean up your ink. If necessary, apply touch-ups with your main weapon to connect your ink. Swim to the top of the wall to rescue the Zapfish.

Stage 03
RISE OF THE OCTOCOPTERS

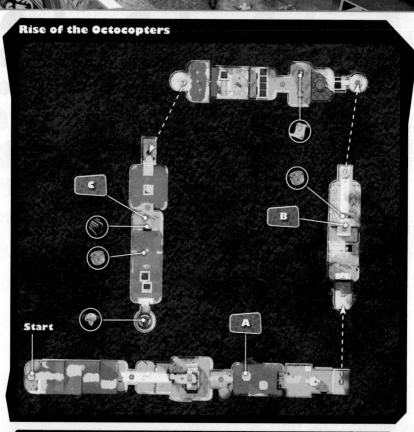

Rise of the Octocopters

C

B

Start

A

Legend

	Key Locations			Armor
	Sunken Scroll			Inkzooka
	Key			Bubbler
	Vault			Bomb Rush
	Zapfish			Jump Path

While in squid form, jump across these two platforms to reach the other side. The tops of the platforms are already coated in your ink, so there's no need to stop. While swimming, you can move faster and jump greater distances. If you fall, ink the sides of one of the platforms and swim back to the top—barriers prevent you from swimming up the perimeter walls.

Smash one of the crates here to acquire an Inkzooka special. Use this powerful weapon to wipe out the distant Octocopters and Octotrooper. The Inkzooka fires a tall tornado of your ink, perfect for eliminating these threats. You have unlimited ammo with the Inkzooka for approximately five seconds—so don't waste too much time aiming. However, each shot fired knocks you back a bit. Be mindful of your footing to avoid getting pushed off the platform or back into a puddle of enemy ink.

Sunken Scroll

The Sunken Scroll is located atop this pillar at the start of the second platform. Swim to the top of the neighboring pillar first. From there, ink the side of the Sunken Scroll's pillar, then jump across in squid form, landing on the pillar's side. Swim to the top of the pillar and bust open the crate to retrieve the Sunken Scroll.

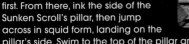

Don't expose yourself to the Octobomber—he throws powerful Splat Bombs. Instead, ink the area around the Octobomber, then swim through your ink to sneak up on him. One of the crates near the center of the platform contains an Inkzooka—grab the Inkzooka, pop out of your ink, and blast the Octobomber before he can respond. The path to the Zapfish is now clear—ink the moving blocks to reach it.

THE MIGHTY OCTOSTOMP

Immediately after jumping to the central platform, don't move forward. Instead, spend some time inking as much of the platform as possible—Seekers are particularly helpful for spreading ink. Spreading your ink around makes it much easier to move about once the battle begins. This allows you to rapidly swim through your ink, making it easier to avoid the boss's stomp attacks.

Round 1

When you're ready to begin the battle, move forward to get the Octostomp's attention. Immediately begin moving laterally in an effort to avoid the first stomp attack—the enemy leaps into the air, and lands face down on the platform. After the Octostomp lands, circle around to one of his sides and begin inking it, drawing a line of ink to his back. Once a path of ink has been created, swim up the side of the Octostomp and immediately open fire on the writhing tentacle on his back—damaging the tentacle is the key to defeating this boss. After damaging the tentacle on the Octostomp's back, a geyser of purple ink erupts from his back—you escape automatically, landing on the platform. Prepare for round two!

40

Round 2

In the second round of the fight, the platform is immediately cleared of all ink. Use your main weapon and sub weapons to spread some ink while avoiding the Octostomp's attacks. Continue using the same plan of attack, dodging his stomp attacks, followed by inking one of his sides while he's face down. This time only portions of his sides can be inked, requiring you to swim up to his back following a zig-zag pattern. Once on his back, target the tentacle to trigger another geyser of purple ink.

Round 3

As the battle enters the third round, follow the same game plan—dodge the Octostomp's attack, and ink one of his sides. However, this time his sides consist of inkable moving panels. These panels are easy enough to ink, but swimming up them can be challenging. Either wait until the panels are aligned, or make a zig-zag ascent to the Octostomp's back. As usual, target the tentacle on his back to defeat the boss

once and for all. After the Octostomp explodes, approach the epicenter of the detonation to collect several Power Eggs, a Sunken Scroll, and an Zapfish.

Ink Battle Rewards

Weapon Unlock: Custom Splattershot Jr.

Now that you've defeated the Octostomp, Sheldon can use the recovered Sunken Scroll to create the Custom Splattershot Jr. Visit Ammo Knights, in the Plaza, to purchase this weapon for 800 gold—it can be used during ink battles.

 ### amiibo Challenges

Defeating the Octostomp during amiibo challenges unlocks new pieces of headgear. These items are automatically added to your inventory and can be equipped for use during ink battles.

amiibo Gear Rewards				
Gear	Name	Rarity	Main Ability	Required amiibo
	Power Mask	⭐⭐	Defense Up	Inkling Squid
	Samurai Helmet	⭐⭐	Damage Up	Inkling Boy
	Squid Hairclip	⭐⭐	Swim Speed Up	Inkling Girl

ZONE 2

Your search for the Great Zapfish continues in this zone, requiring you to fight your way through six Octarian lairs before facing off against the dreaded Octonozzle. Be prepared to use features like Gushers, sponges, and Propeller Lifts to your advantage while advancing through these stages.

Zone 2

Start

06
09
08

05

07

BB

04

Area
Gate

Legend

04	Gusher Gauntlet	08	Octoling Invasion
05	Floating Sponge Garden	09	Unidentified Flying Object
06	Propeller Lift Playground	BB	The Dreaded Octonozzle
07	Spreader Splatfest		

GUSHER GAUNTLET

Gusher Gauntlet

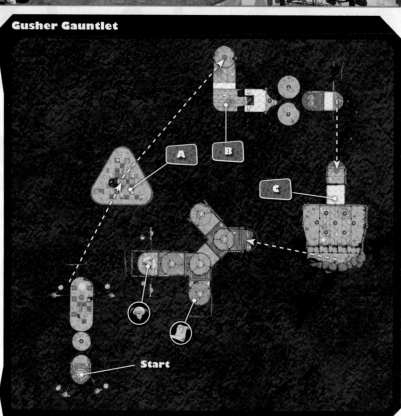

A

B

C

Start

Legend

Key Locations		Armor	
Sunken Scroll		Inkzooka	
Key		Bubbler	
Vault		Bomb Rush	
Zapfish		Jump Path	

A When you land on this platform, you immediately come under fire by three Octotroopers positioned on crates around the perimeter. Immediately drop to the floor of the platform and activate the Gushers. Standing atop a Gusher, you can fire down on the Octotroopers—they'll have no idea where you went. Or simply use the Gushers for cover, peeking around them to fire back at these enemies. Shoot the crates out from beneath the Octotroopers, dropping them to the ground and denying them their height advantage.Balloon Fish in the future to spread ink over large swaths of territory.

B Watch out for the Octostamps here. Just like the Octostomp, these enemies leap forward and land face down, splatting purple ink around them. Sidestep their incoming attacks, then splat them with ink while they're face down. Or if you're feeling mischievous, lure the Octostamps near a ledge, urging them to leap off the side—you'll still earn Power Eggs if they fall.

C An array of seven Gushers awaits you here, as well as five Twintacle Octotroopers. Immediately activate as many Gushers as possible, using the columns of ink for cover and concealment. The Gushers also spread your ink on the platform, allowing you to swim around and flank these enemies, picking them off one by one. Or you can ride to the top of a Gusher and fire down on these Octotroopers. Mobility is key, so keep moving to avoid getting pelted by enemy ink.

Sunken Scroll

This level's Sunken Scroll is located on this tall mesh platform, not far from the Zapfish. Eliminate the Octotrooper standing atop the crate, then move in to grab the Sunken Scroll.

Stage 05
FLOATING SPONGE GARDEN

Floating Sponge Garden

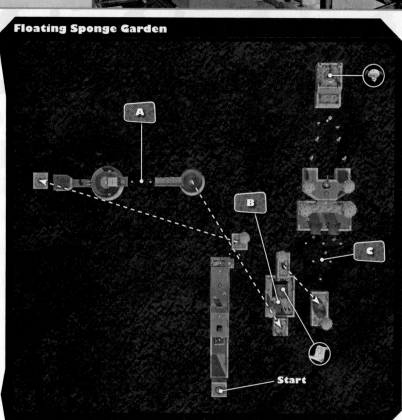

A

B

C

Start

Legend

Key Locations		Armor	
Sunken Scroll		Inkzooka	
Key		Bubbler	
Vault		Bomb Rush	
Zapfish		Jump Path	

46

Ink these three sponges and walk across them. But watch out for the three Octoballs that appear ahead. Instead of shooting them, simply retreat to the center sponge. As the Octoballs chase you across the first sponge, their ink causes the sponge to shrink—eventually they'll fall, netting you Power Eggs without even firing a shot. This is an important lesson—enemy ink causes sponges to shrink!

 The large blue sponge here has already absorbed your ink. You need to get it to shrink. Eliminate the two Octopods around the base, then swim to the top of the sponge, luring the two Octotroopers above to fire down at you. Dodge their incoming fire, allowing it to hit the sponge. As the sponge shrinks, a cargo net is revealed beneath it—just below this net is a hidden platform holding the level's Sunken Scroll.

Sunken Scroll

 After the sponge has been shrunk, drop through the cargo net in squid form to access this platform where the Sunken Scroll is waiting in a crate. If you can't shrink the sponge above, you can still access this platform. Walk off the side of the platform above, and drift toward this platform as you fall.

 Crossing this array of sponges is risky, due to the three Octocopters and Twintacle Octotrooper waiting on the other side. Stay hidden in your ink until you reach the second set of sponges in the middle—the Octocopters are now in range. Engage the Octocopters one by one. If you come under fire, stay near the center of the sponge, as this is the safest place to stand as the sponge shrinks. Continue to the third set of sponges and engage the patrolling Twintacle Octotrooper on the neighboring platform. Just ahead, use the Ink Cannon to blast your way through the remaining opposition.

PROPELLER LIFT PLAYGROUND

Propeller Lift Playground

Start

Legend

	Key Locations		Armor
	Sunken Scroll		Inkzooka
	Key		Bubbler
	Vault		Bomb Rush
	Zapfish		Jump Path

Stand on the center Propeller Lift and shoot the propeller to begin your ascent. As the lift rises, open fire on the five Octotroopers below. Don't worry too much about incoming fire. The Propeller Lift slowly descends, making you a moving target the Octotroopers can't hit. But occasionally target the propeller to give the lift more altitude, maintaining a height advantage over the doomed Octotroopers.

Sunken Scroll

 Don't stand on the Propeller Lift here. Instead, stand aside and shoot the propeller, causing it to rise. Drop through the hole beneath the Propeller Lift to access this hidden platform, containing the level's Sunken Scroll. Use the launchpad to return to the platform above.

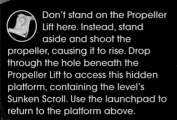

 Remember, you can't swim. So exercise caution when navigating this water feature. Use the two Propeller Lifts to cross this area while engaging Octocopters and Octotroopers. Maintain constant movement to avoid becoming a sitting duck. When you reach the Shielded Octotrooper on the last platform, use a Splat Bomb to divert his attention. Toss it behind him so he exposes his back to you. Alternatively, you can ink the area around him and swim behind him for a rear sneak attack.

Here Octotroopers occupy a couple of Propeller Lifts. Target the propellers to get these lifts moving—this decreases the accuracy of the Octotroopers as they open fire. Return fire or toss a Splat Bomb atop each platform. Once clear, check the sides and bottoms of each platform for Power Eggs. Simply shoot the Power Eggs to collect them. Ride the second Propeller Lift up to rescue the Zapfish.

Stage 07
SPREADER SPLATFEST

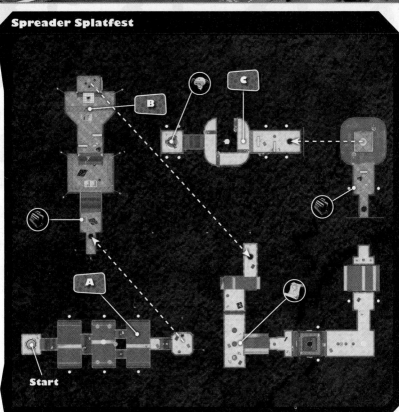

Spreader Splatfest

A

B

C

Start

Legend

	Key Locations		Armor
	Sunken Scroll		Inkzooka
	Key		Bubbler
	Vault		Bomb Rush
	Zapfish		Jump Path

 As their name implies, Spreaders cover large areas with purple ink, erasing your ink in the process. Instead of firing ink across these areas and trying to race ahead, avoid the Spreaders. Simply ride atop the Spreaders while crossing these areas. You can even ink the top of the Spreaders, and hide in your ink. But there's an Octotrooper already riding the third Spreader in this area—splat him and then step onto the Spreader to cross.

 Watch out for the Octodiver hiding in the purple ink at the base of this wall. These enemies remain submerged in their ink until you approach, attempting to ambush you. Either target the Octodiver directly or hit the Balloon Fish on the Spreader above to rain down your ink. Afterward, make sure the Spreader is coated in your ink, then swim up the Spreader (or wall) to reach the next launchpad.

Sunken Scroll

The Sunken Scroll is located just beneath the main platform, in the area patrolled by two Octocopters. Step onto one of the nearby Spreaders, then turn around to locate this hidden area. Step off the Spreader and smash the crate to retrieve the level's Sunken Scroll.

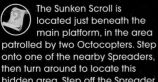

 There are four Octotroopers (including one Shielded Octotrooper) guarding these Spreaders in front of the Zapfish. Stay behind cover to avoid being detected, then step out to shoot the Balloon Fish in the center. The resulting explosion of your ink is powerful enough to take out a couple of the enemies, including the troublesome Shielded Octotrooper. Stay behind cover and throw Splat Bombs at the remaining enemies, tossing the bombs just ahead of the Spreader the enemies are riding on. This clears the path to the Zapfish.

Octoling Invasion

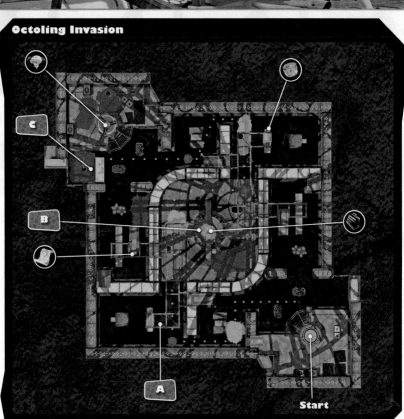

C

B

A

Start

Legend

Key Locations		Armor	
Sunken Scroll		Inkzooka	
Key		Bubbler	
Vault		Bomb Rush	
Zapfish		Jump Path	

A You can take any path you'd like through this maze-like level, but watch out for enemies. The Octolings you encounter on this stage are dangerous and intelligent. In addition to aggressively attacking you, they'll hide in their ink and occasionally toss Splat Bombs in your direction—all of this is excellent training for ink battles. To avoid getting splatted, take the high ground offered by the catwalk. You can fire down through the mesh floor of the catwalk to hit Octolings below. However, if you turn into squid form, you'll fall through the mesh floor, potentially landing in enemy ink.

B Once on the catwalk, rush the cylindrical platform in the center. The large crate here contains armor. Armor is vital during battles with Octolings, helping prevent you from getting splatted—the armor takes the damage instead of you. The top of this platform can also be inked, allowing you to hide in your ink and replenish your ink tank. So if you're on the catwalk and need ink, move to this platform to reload. This is an ideal spot for raining down ink and Splat Bombs on the Octolings below.

Sunken Scroll

 The level's Sunken Scroll is hidden behind this ramp leading up to the catwalk—not far from the Zapfish. Be sure to grab it before completing the level.

C You must use a couple of Inkrails to reach the Zapfish here. But before making a move for the Inkrails, make sure the area is clear of Octolings. In this fight, you're likely at a height disadvantage. Instead of firing up at the Octolings, stay behind cover and lob Splat Bombs onto the upper platform—this is a good area to use the level's Inkzooka as well. When you've splatted all Octolings here, traverse the Inkrails to grab the Zapfish.

Stage 09
UNIDENTIFIED FLYING OBJECT

Unidentified Flying Object

Start

C

B

A

Legend

	Key Locations		Armor
	Sunken Scroll		Inkzooka
	Key		Bubbler
	Vault		Bomb Rush
	Zapfish		Jump Path

A Advance through this area as quickly as possible. The Octostriker on the hovering flying saucer continually attacks with Inkstrikes— these are massive, lethal tornados of purple ink. Keep moving to avoid getting caught up in one of these Inkstrikes. When possible, swim through your ink in squid form to avoid getting spotted by the Octostriker. While avoiding Inkstrikes, be on watch for Octodivers hiding in the purple ink. Grab the armor here before moving on.

Sunken Scroll

 After eliminating the Octodiver near the Gusher, smash the crate beneath this yellow bridge to reveal the level's Sunken Scroll.

 B Already drenched in purple ink, this area is also home to several Octodivers lurking just beneath the surface. Ink the ground as you move through this area, eliminating Octodivers as you go. Ink coverage is important here because you'll need somewhere to swim to when Inkstrikes appear. Use Splat Bombs or Seekers to expand ink coverage here, giving you more options for escape.

 C Pursue the Octostriker around the edge of the flying saucer while splatting Octocopters along the way. The Octocopters continually respawn here, so don't worry about taking them all out. Instead, focus on inking the perimeter of the flying saucer, then swim through your ink to get close to the Octostriker—he will continue backing up while launching Inkstrikes. When you're within range, continually pelt the Octostriker with ink until he explodes. If you attack aggressively, you can take him out within a matter of seconds. You can then retrieve the Zapfish from the center of the flying saucer.

THE DREADED OCTONOZZLE

As you did during your fight with the Octostomp, spend some time spreading ink around the platform before approaching the boss. As long as you don't move forward, you can spend as much time as you like expanding your ink coverage. Seekers are particularly useful for creating ink trails across the platform. Focus on coating the area surrounding the boss. This will help out considerably during the first round of the battle.

Round 1

As the battle begins, swim forward through your ink and go on the offensive. Take note of the exposed tentacle poking out of the porthole—this is your target. But don't forget to avoid the purple balls of ink fired from the boss's nose. These balls of purple ink roll across the platform, inflicting heavy damage if they hit you. When you're not dodging these balls, resume your attack on the exposed tentacle. Once you've done enough damage, the Octonozzle stops its attacks and a large tentacle pokes out of its head. Ink the side of the Octonozzle, swim to the top, and shoot the tentacle until it explodes.

Round 2

In the second round, the platform is cleared of all ink, so ink a path toward the Octonozzle to resume your attack. This time the boss occasionally fires a wide spread of purple ink balls. These are much more difficult to avoid, especially if you're not close to the boss. So stay close, keeping the area around the Octonozzle inked while firing at the two newly exposed tentacles poking out of the portholes on the front and back of the enemy.

After destroying the tentacle on the front, circle around the Octonozzle and target the exposed tentacle on its back. Continue circling the Octonozzle and hitting this weak spot until the boss stops and a large tentacle pokes out of its head—this is your cue to swim to the top and splat the wiggling tentacle.

Round 3

As the final round gets underway, rush toward the Octonozzle and ink the area around him while targeting the four exposed tentacles. This requires you to circle around the Octonozzle to hit all four of these targets—swim around the perimeter to avoid getting smacked by incoming ink balls. Once all four tentacles are destroyed, the Octonozzle stops and exposes its large tentacle one last time. Swim to the top and splat the writhing tentacle to defeat the boss. In the aftermath, collect several Power Eggs and the Sunken Scroll before rescuing the Zapfish.

Ink Battle Rewards

Weapon Unlock: Kelp Splat Charger

Now that you've defeated the Octonozzle, Sheldon can use the recovered Sunken Scroll to create the Kelp Splat Charger. Visit Ammo Knights, in the Plaza, to purchase this weapon for 2,500 gold—it can be used during ink battles.

amiibo Challenges

Defeating the Octonozzle during amiibo challenges unlocks new clothing. These items are automatically added to your inventory and can be equipped for use during ink battles.

amiibo Gear Rewards

Gear	Name	Rarity	Main Ability	Required amiibo
	Power Armor	⭐⭐	Quick Respawn	Inkling Squid
	Samurai Jacket	⭐⭐	Special Recovery Up	Inkling Boy
	School Uniform	⭐⭐	Ink Recovery Up	Inkling Girl

ZONE 3

Despite your efforts in the previous zones, the Octarians aren't prepared to give up the Great Zapfish. This requires you to infiltrate six more lairs, culminating in a battle with the rampaging Octowhirl. Along the way, work on mastering Inkrails, particularly when it comes to accessing this zone's scattered lairs.

Zone 3

Start

11

10

13

BB

12

14

15

Area
Gate

Legend

10	Inkrail Skyscape	**14**	Octoling Assault
11	Inkvisible Avenues	**15**	Undeniable Flying Object
12	Flooder Junkyard	**BB**	The Rampaging Octowhirl

Stage 10
INKRAIL SKYSCAPE

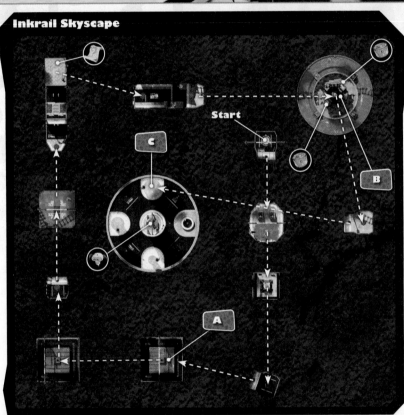

Inkrail Skyscape

Start

A

B

C

Legend

Key Locations		Armor	
Sunken Scroll		Inkzooka	
Key		Bubbler	
Vault		Bomb Rush	
Zapfish		Jump Path	

When advancing across these adjoining platforms, build up speed along the Inkrail, then jump toward the center of the platform. Speed is essential for reaching the center, launching your squid high into the air. But watch out for enemies—the first platform is patrolled by a lone Octotrooper.

Two Octodivers are hiding on the second platform. So immediately after jumping, return to Inkling form and open fire on the enemies.

Sunken Scroll

 When you reach the wall with three parallel Inkrails, jump to the middle Inkrail and follow it around the back of the platform. This leads to a hidden area where you can retrieve the level's Sunken Scroll.

 On this platform you're completely surrounded by eight Octotroopers. Fortunately, there are two Inkzookas nearby to help you out of this tight spot. Grab one of the Inkzookas, then duck behind one of the ramps in the center of the platform for cover. Activate the Inkzooka and peek out of cover while rapidly

targeting the Octotroopers. There's no need to save these Inkzookas, so you might as well use them both here. Splat as many Octotroopers as possible with the first Inkzooka, then grab the other one and continue firing.

 Ride the Inkrail to the final platform. Each of the three pillars are connected by Inkrails—they're also guarded by Octotroopers. Speed along the Inkrail toward each pillar, then jump before the Inkrail terminates. If you jump while moving along the Inkrail at high speed, you'll launch yourself high into the

air, flying above the Octotrooper. While in mid-air, aim down and open fire on the Octotrooper before you land. If you act quickly, you can splat the Octotroopers before they can retaliate. Continue along the Inkrails until you reach the Zapfish in the center.

Stage 11
INKVISIBLE AVENUES

Inkvisible Avenues

A

B

C

Start

Legend

Key Locations		Armor	
Sunken Scroll		Inkzooka	
Key		Bubbler	
Vault		Bomb Rush	
Zapfish		Jump Path	

As the name implies, many of the paths and walls on this level are invisible. However, you can uncover these hidden features by coating them with your ink. Start by shooting the Balloon Fish here to spread ink over the two invisible paths. But watch out ahead—there's an Octoling and Octocopter guarding the neighboring platform. Ink the invisible walls to identify points of cover, then use Splat Bombs to take out the enemies.

Sunken Scroll

From the second platform's launchpad, look down and off the side, and fire ink to discover an invisible platform below. Drop down onto the platform to find the level's Sunken Scroll, hidden beneath this ramp.

Take it nice and slow in this area. The invisible path here is extremely narrow, so ink a little bit at a time while inching forward. Be on watch for Octocopters appearing above—deal with these threats as quickly as possible, as you have very little room to maneuver. The Squee-Gs on this path are less of an issue—just move past them as quickly as possible. But watch out for the Octobomber appearing near the end of the path, near the launchpad. The Octobomber's incoming Splat Bombs are a serious problem, so deal with this threat before he can throw any.

The path to the Zapfish consists of several invisible terraced steps, each occupied by Twintacle Octotroopers. Fortunately, each step has invisible walls you can hide behind. Ink these walls and take cover behind them while tossing Splat Bombs toward the Octotroopers. Alternatively, peek out of cover long enough to fire some ink toward these threats. After clearing all visible threats, enter squid form and jump to the next step. Keep working your way up through this area until you can secure the Zapfish.

Stage 12
FLOODER JUNKYARD

Flooder Junkyard

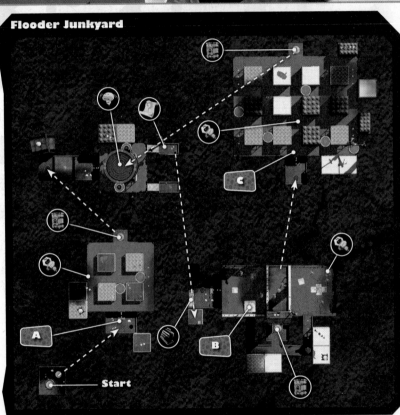

A

B

C

Start

Legend

🟦	Key Locations	⚫	Armor
🌀	Sunken Scroll	🔵	Inkzooka
🔑	Key	🔵	Bubbler
📦	Vault	🔵	Bomb Rush
⚡	Zapfish	➤	Jump Path

A Two Flooders patrol this platform, constantly spreading ink. Flooders can't be destroyed, so you need to avoid them. Ink your way along the left side of the platform to retrieve the key, then continue to the vault at the back of the platform. To avoid being spotted by a Flooder, stay in squid form and swim through your ink.

Seekers come in handy here, creating narrow, linear trails of ink for you to swim through.

Sunken Scroll

 Veer right on the second platform to access an Inkrail leading down to this level's Sunken Scroll.

 B This platform is swarming with Octodivers and Twintacle Octotroopers—retrieve the armor before advancing any further. Destroy the crates here to reveal a mesh opening in the floor. Enter squid form to drop through the mesh to access a lower walkway. From here you can access the

platform's vault–the key is located in the adjoining Octodiver-infested area. The vault unlocks a propeller-lift leading to the platform's launchpad. But deal with the two Twintacle Octotroopers guarding the launchpad first.

 C This large grid-like area is patrolled by five Flooders. You must search this area for a lone Octodiver carrying a key. Use Seekers to rapidly ink narrow paths for you to swim through—this is also a good method for uncovering the hidden Octodiver. Be aware of the surrounding Flooders and

make sure you have a path of escape, even if it means returning to the platform's checkpoint. Once you've recovered the key, make your way toward the vault. The vault reveals an Inkrail leading directly to the Zapfish.

Tip

There are two balloons located directly beneath the Zapfish's platform. Drop down from the Inkrail to splat these balloons. You can then use the Gushers atop the two patrolling Flooders to return to the Zapfish's platform.

Stage 13
SHIFTING SPLATFORMS

Shifting Splatforms

Start

Legend

	Key Locations		Armor
	Sunken Scroll		Inkzooka
	Key		Bubbler
	Vault		Bomb Rush
	Zapfish		Jump Path

Watch your step as you advance across these shifting platforms here. Ink the floor of each platform before stepping aboard. As the platform shifts beneath the net, hide in your ink to avoid getting scraped off. As if this isn't challenging enough, you come under attack by several Octocopters and Octotroopers in this area. Even as you're under attack, be ready to duck under that net—it poses a bigger threat than the Octarians. Try to eliminate as many of these threats from the non-shifting platforms as you can.

Sunken Scroll

Before climbing the shifting blocks on the third platform, follow the narrow path to the right to locate this level's Sunken Scroll.

This obstacle consists of three moving blocks. Thoroughly ink these blocks before attempting to swim up them. The glass and blue tarp sections cannot be inked, so you must rely on inking the metal surfaces to make your way to the top. As you transition from the second moving block to the third one, you must act fast. Swim up the non-tarp side of the second block, then immediately ink and swim up the side of the third block—stay in squid form when you reach the top to avoid getting scraped off by the net.

Swimming up the three moving sections of this final wall can be tricky. First, ink all three moving sections of the wall. Swim up the first section and remain there until you can swim to the second section. Gravity continually pushes your squid downward, so you need to keep swimming up gradually to stay in one spot on the wall. Be patient and keep swimming upward, one section at a time, until you reach the top. But beware of the net waiting for you here—ink the floor and hide in your ink to avoid getting scraped off. Swim up the adjoining wall to reach the Zapfish.

Stage 14
OCTOLING ASSAULT

Octoling Assault

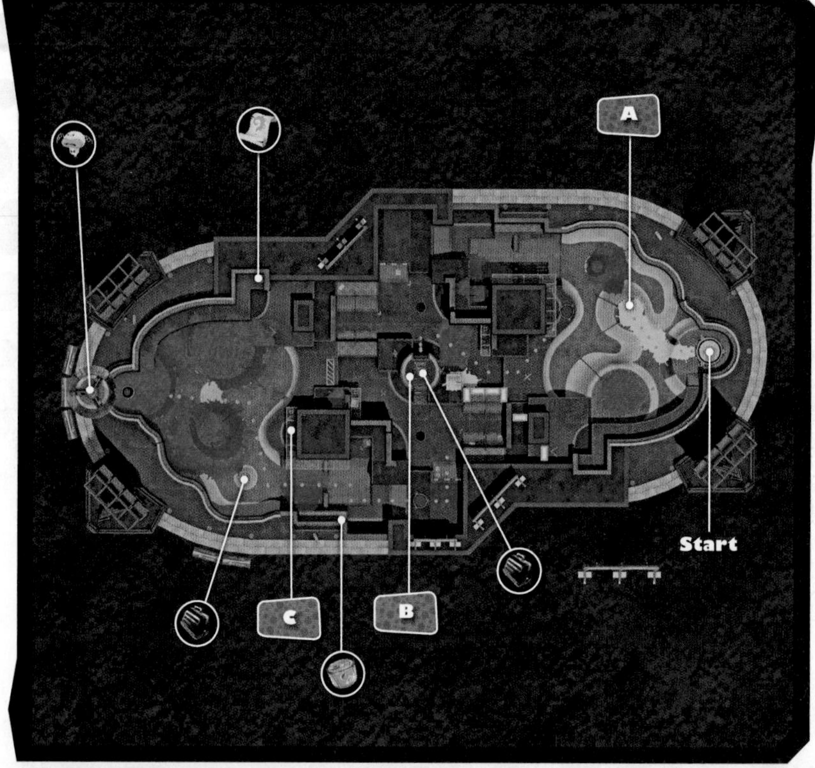

Legend

Key Locations	Armor
Sunken Scroll	Inkzooka
Key	Bubbler
Vault	Bomb Rush
Zapfish	Jump Path

This stage should look familiar if you've competed in ink battles on Blackbelly Skatepark. Follow the line of Power Eggs leading out of the start point, but watch out for Octolings in the pool section ahead. Instead of diving down into the pool area, remain on the high ground, firing down on the Octolings below.

Your height advantage makes it harder for them to target you with their Splat Bombs. Maintain the high ground until this area is clear of Octolings.

 Get to this central tower as quickly as possible, even if it means swimming away from Octolings. Ink one of the ramps on the side of the tower and swim to the top, retrieving the armor in the crate. From this high perch you have a commanding view of the entire skatepark, ideal for picking

off Octolings scurrying about below. Aim high to arc your ink (and Splat Bombs) great distances.

 Swim up to this yellow catwalk overlooking the next pool area. Once again, use the height advantage to fire down on the Octolings below. If you grabbed the Inkzooka, use it to spread your ink across this area, cutting off Octoling escape paths. Be careful not to turn into squid form while on

this catwalk—you'll fall through the mesh. If you need to replenish your ink tank, ink the wall adjacent to the catwalk and swim along the wall. When you can no longer see any Octolings, cautiously cross the pool area and activate the Gusher to reach the Zapfish—if any Octolings remain, you can target them from the Zapfish's platform.

Sunken Scroll

 Before using the Gusher, follow this narrow path to the right to locate the level's Sunken Scroll.

Stage 15
UNDENIABLE FLYING OBJECT

Undeniable Flying Object

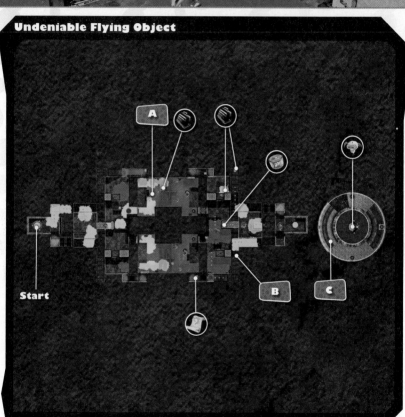

A

B

C

Start

Legend

Key Locations		Armor	
Sunken Scroll		Inkzooka	
Key		Bubbler	
Vault		Bomb Rush	
Zapfish		Jump Path	

On this stage, an Octostriker is positioned on the distant flying saucer and continually attacks with Inkstrikes. So swim through your ink as much as possible to avoid being spotted by the Octostriker. Veer left to take this path toward the flying saucer. Grab the armor in the crate, then engage two Twintacle Octotroopers and an Octobomber. Conveniently, the Octobomber is hovering just below a Gusher—all Octobombers in this stage are positioned over Gushers. Activate the Gushers to instantly splat these Splat Bomb-tossing threats.

Sunken Scroll

 After reaching this checkpoint, turn around and smash this crate to retrieve the level's Sunken Scroll.

B This narrow walkway is extremely dangerous. While crossing the mesh catwalk, be careful not to turn into squid form—you'll fall through and drop into the water below. Since you can't swim along the catwalk, expect an incoming Inkstrike, not to mention incoming Splat Bombs tossed by an Octobomber. Do your best to dodge the Inkstrike, then activate the Gusher beneath the Octobomber. Grab the nearby Bubbler and stock up on armor before heading for the flying saucer.

C As you did in the last fight against an Octostriker, ink the perimeter of the flying saucer, then swim to close range. If you haven't already, this is a good time to activate the Bubbler special. This makes you invincible for a few seconds, allowing you to solely focus on offense. Target the Gushers along the perimeter of the flying saucer to splat the pesky Octocopters. But try to stay focused on the Octostriker, continually splatting him with ink until he explodes. Following the fight, retrieve the Zapfish from the center of the flying saucer to complete this stage.

Boss Battle
THE RAMPAGING
OCTOWHIRL

Before charging toward the boss, take a moment to spread some ink across the platform. This will allow you to maneuver with ease during the first round of the battle. After landing on the platform, don't move forward. Instead coat the floor around you and toss Seekers to create ink trails across the platform.

Round 1

The rampaging Octowhirl is a large, metal sphere that spins across the platform like a top, spreading purple ink. During this phase of its attack, just avoid it. Keep an eye on its movement while spreading ink across the center of the platform. But when the Octowhirl stops, pay close attention. At this point the Octowhirl comes rolling toward you at high speed. Enter squid mode and be ready to jump out of its way. If there's enough of your ink in its path, the rolling Octowhirl gets bogged down and comes to a sudden stop—here's your chance to attack. When the Octowhirl gets stuck in your ink, splat the wiggling tentacle sticking out of the top of the sphere to advance the battle to the next round.

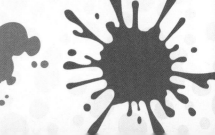

Round 2

At the start of the second round, the platform is cleared of ink and the Octowhirl's speed increases. A ring, adjacent to the center of the platform, also begins rotating. Move to the center of the platform and thoroughly ink the area around you, including most of the rotating ring. When the Octowhirl stops, enter squid mode and be ready to jump out of the way as it comes rolling at you—leap laterally, at a perpendicular angle to the incoming Octowhirl, to avoid getting splatted. The Octowhirl's increased speed makes it much tougher to dodge this time. However, if you've spread enough ink in its path, it will get bogged down and come to a sudden stop. Target the writhing tentacle once again to reset the Octowhirl, and enter the third phase of the battle.

Round 3

In the third round, the ink is cleared from the platform and the Octowhirl's speed increases even more. This time the platform undergoes some drastic changes too, with large sections composed of glass, which cannot be inked. With fewer inkable surfaces, it becomes more difficult to slow down the Octowhirl when it comes rolling at you. Stay in the center and keep inking as much of the platform as possible while dodging the Octowhirl's roll attacks. Eventually the Octowhirl will roll through enough green ink to get bogged down. Target the wiggling tentacle one last time to defeat the Octowhirl, causing it to explode. Gather the Power Eggs and Sunken Scroll left behind before retrieving the Zapfish.

Ink Battle Rewards

Weapon Unlock: Aerospray MG & Aerospray RG

Using the Sunken Scroll retrieved from the Rampaging Octowhirl, Sheldon can now create the rapid-firing Aerospray MG and Aerospray RG. These weapons can be purchased from Ammo Knights once you've reached level 7 and level 13, respectively.

 amiibo Challenges

Defeating the Octowhirl during amiibo challenges unlocks new shoes. You can equip these items for use during ink battles.

amiibo Gear Rewards				
Gear	Name	Rarity	Main Ability	Required amiibo
	Power Boots	⭐⭐	Ink Saver (Main)	Inkling Squid
	Samurai Shoes	⭐⭐	Special Duration Up	Inkling Boy
	School Shoes	⭐⭐	Ink Saver (Sub)	Inkling Girl

ZONE 4

Cap'n Cuttlefish reports that progress is being made in the fight against the Octarians. After introducing you to Agents 1 and 2, Cap'n Cuttlefish is abducted by some unknown threat. Fight your way through six more lairs to reach the Octomaw. Perhaps defeating this boss will yield more clues on Cap'n Cuttlefish's whereabouts?

Zone 4

19

20

BB

18

Start

21

17

16

Area Gate

Legend

16	Propeller-Lift Fortress	20	Octoling Uprising
17	Octosniper Ramparts	21	Unwelcome Flying Object
18	Spinning Spreaders	BB	The Ravenous Octomaw
19	Tumbling Splatforms		

Note

Lairs 16, 18, and 19 are located on small platforms beneath this zone. Use the Inkrail system beneath the zone to access these lairs.

Stage 16
PROPELLER-LIFT FORTRESS

Propeller-Lift Fortress

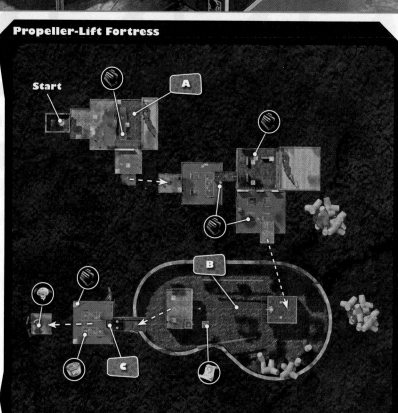

Start

A

B

C

Legend

	Key Locations		Armor
	Sunken Scroll		Inkzooka
	Key		Bubbler
	Vault		Bomb Rush
	Zapfish		Jump Path

Ascending this retractable wall can be a bit tricky. Target the propeller to cause the wall to extend, allowing you to climb it. Before swimming up this feature, thoroughly ink it and make sure the wall is extended to its fullest. Swim along the inked wall sections before the wall retracts, causing you to fall.

You'll need to move fast if you want to grab the armor up top. Also, watch out for the Twintacle Octotrooper patrolling the adjacent area.

 Use the Ink Cannon to shoot the Propeller Lift, then hop on board—use the Ink Cannon to completely coat the lift with your ink while you're at it. While riding the Propeller Lift across the water, watch out for Octocopters appearing above. Eliminate these threats as soon as they appear, swimming

through your ink as necessary to avoid incoming fire. There's also an Octobomer who appears near the end of the ride. Target the propeller on the lift to cause the platform to reverse direction, making you a more difficult target for these enemies.

Sunken Scroll

 While riding the Propeller Lift across the water, ink the tall section of the approaching wall. When you're close enough, jump to the wall and swim up it. Once atop the wall, turn around to locate this level's Sunken Scroll, in the crate.

 Pause on this ledge before dropping down—there are two Octolings waiting to ambush you. Take a moment to spread some ink in the area below and plan your attack. After dropping off the ledge, make a move for the Bubbler special located on the Propeller Lift to the left. Once you get the Bubbler, activate it and aggressively hunt down the two Octolings while you're invincible. Alternatively, activate one of the two Propeller Lift platforms to get a height advantage on the Octolings. Once the area is clear, use the launchpad to reach the Zapfish.

Stage 17
OCTOSNIPER RAMPARTS

Octosniper Ramparts

B

A

Start

C

Legend

	Key Locations		Armor
	Sunken Scroll		Inkzooka
	Key		Bubbler
	Vault		Bomb Rush
	Zapfish		Jump Path

This stage introduces a new enemy: the Octosniper. As their name suggests, these are long-range specialists capable of firing accurate streams of ink great distances. You'll need to move in close before you can hit these guys. So stay behind cover or hidden in your ink to avoid being targeted—

keep an eye on the Octosniper's green targeting laser to determine which way he's looking. Seekers are a great way to distract Octosnipers, causing them to turn and follow the device until it explodes, so use Seekers as distractions. Stealthily sneak up on this first Octosniper until you can get close enough to take him out with a Splat Bomb.

 There are three Octosnipers watching this area, including two on the distant moving platform. When the distant Octosnipers have moved out of sight, sneak up on the lone Octosniper, near the cargo net, and take him out. Continue toward the moving platform, eliminating the Octotrooper along the way. When

you're close enough to the moving platform, stay behind cover and bombard it with Splat Bombs until both Octosnipers are eliminated.

Sunken Scroll

 Once the Octosnipers have been eliminated, return to the cargo net and drop through in squid form to locate this level's Sunken Scroll.

 The ramps here are watched by four Octosnipers and two Octotroopers. You're at a severe height disadvantage here, so take it slow. Stay behind cover and use Splat Bombs and Seekers to ink a path ahead. Seekers are great for creating narrow ink trails up the ramps. Ink your way closer and

closer to each enemy until you can swim right next to them and splat them. Or if you prefer, stay behind cover and hit them indirectly with Splat Bombs. Keep inching your way along these ramps until you reach the Zapfish.

Stage 18
SPINNING SPREADERS

Spinning Spreaders

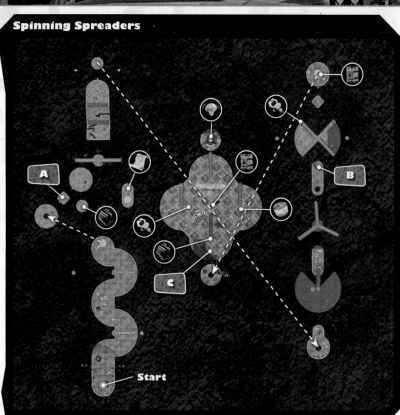

A

B

C

Start

Legend

	Key Locations			Armor
	Sunken Scroll			Inkzooka
	Key			Bubbler
	Vault			Bomb Rush
	Zapfish			Jump Path

There isn't much room to maneuver on these small platforms, so try to eliminate the Octocopters as quickly as possible. Ink a path ahead, then enter squid form, jumping from one platform to the next, collecting the armor along the way. Ink the tops of the two Spreaders and ride them, hiding in your ink until you're close enough to engage the remaining Octocopters.

Sunken Scroll

After clearing out the Octocopters, ride the long Spreader toward this isolated platform. Ink the side of the approaching platform, then swim and jump toward it to reach the level's Sunken Scroll.

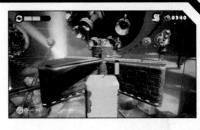

Ink the top of this narrow pillar and hide in your ink while watching the nearby Spreader. Ambush the two Twintacle Octotroopers riding on the Spreader as they approach—pop out of your ink, open fire, then drop back into your ink. One of these Octotroopers has the key to the vault. Once both Octotroopers are eliminated, collect the dropped key from the Spreader, then carefully ink a path to the vault, swimming and jumping along the adjacent platform and pillar.

Before dropping down onto this platform, take a moment to spread some ink. As soon as you drop down, the Spreaders begin rotating, creating large circles of purple ink. To make matters worse, you come under attack by two Octolings—one after another. Make a beeline for the armor in the nearby crate, then confront the Octolings. If possible, make it to the Bomb Rush special on the right side of the platform. This allows you to throw unlimited Splat Bombs, Burst Bombs, and Seekers for a few seconds. This can come in handy during your fight against the Octolings. The second Octoling drops the key to the vault. Open the vault to access an Inkrail leading to the Zapfish.

Stage 19
TUMBLING SPLATFORMS

Tumbling Splatforms

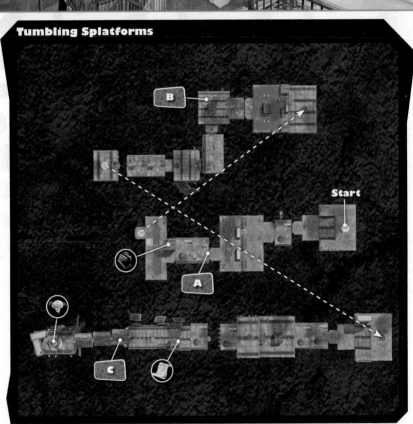

Legend

Key Locations		Armor	
Sunken Scroll		Inkzooka	
Key		Bubbler	
Vault		Bomb Rush	
Zapfish		Jump Path	

This level is filled with rotating platforms, requiring some finesse and attention to detail. This platform rotates clockwise. So when you hop on it, you need to continually sidestep to the left to stay on top. It's not a bad idea to ink the platform as well, giving you the ability to swim through the ink if the platform becomes too vertical for you to stand on. When the platform rotates to its most vertical position, cross the top and jump to the nearby shipping container where you can obtain some armor. Fire down on the Twintacle Octotrooper below and proceed to the launchpad.

When you encounter this Octobomber, hide behind these blue storage tanks to avoid being spotted. Instead of attacking the Octobomber directly, toss a Splat Bomb over the tanks to take him out. Beyond the Octobomber are two large blocks, both rotating counter-clockwise. Ink the sides of these blocks and sidestep right while crossing them. From the second block, ink the nearby wall and squid jump over to it to reach the next checkpoint.

Sunken Scroll

After dropping off the yellow grate, turn around to spot these crates tucked away in a hidden alcove. The orange crate contains this level's Sunken Scroll.

These three rotating platforms are the trickiest to ascend. Ink the side of the first platform, then when it rotates to a vertical position, enter squid form and swim up the side to reach the top. Sidestep right along the platform while inking the side of the second platform. When the two platforms are aligned vertically, swim up the side of the second platform. Keep continuing in this fashion with the third platform until you can reach the Zapfish on the high perch ahead.

Stage 20
OCTOLING UPRISING

Octoling Uprising

C

A

B

Start

Legend

	Key Locations			Armor
	Sunken Scroll			Inkzooka
	Key			Bubbler
	Vault			Bomb Rush
	Zapfish			Jump Path

If this stage looks familiar, it's because it's identical to the one you cleared in Udeniable Flying Object. This time you don't have to worry about an Octostriker—just Octolings. Take your time clearing out the Octolings on this side of the stage. This elevated perch is an ideal position, allowing you to fire

down on the enemies below. Lob Burst Bombs and Splat Bombs onto the Octolings until the area is clear. Then drop down and claim the armor in the nearby crate before proceeding to the first checkpoint.

After grabbing the nearby Bomb Rush special, pause near the first checkpoint and engage the Octoling below. If you'd like, use Bomb Rush to saturate the area below with Splat Bombs. There's an identical perch to the right, perfect for firing down on a second Octoling located across the water

feature in the center of the stage. You can also use the perimeter perches, near where you found the Bomb Rush special. Use these elevated positons to engage the Octolings in these two lower areas.

Two Octolings wait to ambush you here. Take care when ascending the mesh ramp—if you enter squid form while on this ramp, you'll fall in the water. For best results, use Bubbler while rushing toward the checkpoint and the nearby Inkrail. Use the Inkrail to cross this area, moving toward the crate containing

armor. Once you've established a foothold, use Splat Bombs and your Hero Shot to clear out the Octolings. When both Octolings are eliminated, proceed to the next Inkrail to retrieve the Zapfish.

Sunken Scroll

Before using the Inkrail leading to the Zapfish, drop through the nearby mesh ramp by entering squid form. Just below this ramp is a crate containing the level's Sunken Scroll.

Stage 21
UNWELCOME FLYING OBJECT

Unwelcome Flying Object

C

A

B

Start

Legend

Key Locations		Armor	
Sunken Scroll		Inkzooka	
Key		Bubbler	
Vault		Bomb Rush	
Zapfish		Jump Path	

86

Another Octostriker overlooks this stage from the safety of his flying saucer, so don't linger in any one spot for very long to avoid getting targeted with an Inkstrike. A small army of Octocopters and Octotroopers have established a blockade in the center of the stage. Grab the Inkzooka and open

fire. The tornados of ink fired by the Inkzooka are perfect for clearing a path. The tornados of ink are even tall enough to take out the hovering Octocopters. But while firing, be on watch for an incoming Inkstrike—and be ready to move.

 Two Octobombers block the launchpad leading to the flying saucer. Move quickly to get past these threats. Swim up the inked sponge and grab the Bomb Rush special. Immediately toss a Splat Bomb between the two Octobombers to take them out. If

you hesitate here too long, an Inkstrike or Splat Bombs tossed by the Octobombers will cause the sponge to shrink. So it's important to complete this attack quickly to avoid getting bogged down around the sponge.

Sunken Scroll

 After taking out the two Octobombers by the launchpad, backtrack to this perimeter corridor—it's guarded by another Octobomber. Rush the Octobomber and take him out. Just behind him is a crate containing the level's Sunken Scroll.

 When it's time to take the fight to the Octostriker, consider using the Inkrail on the inside track of the flying saucer. The Inkrail allows you to rapidly charge the Octostriker. When you're close, hop off the Inkrail and shoot up at the Octostriker until he explodes. During the fight, don't neglect

the Octotroopers on the perimeter of the flying saucer. But as long as you keep moving, they shouldn't be much of a threat. Once the fight is over, retrieve the Zapfish from the center of the flying saucer.

THE RAVENOUS OCTOMAW

As you've done in all previous boss battles, take a moment to thoroughly ink the platform before approaching the Octomaw. After landing on the platform, use your Hero Shot, Splat Bombs, and Seekers to ink as much territory as possible. The more ink spread, the easier it is to swim across the platform and avoid the Octomaw's attacks.

Round 1

As you approach the center of the platform, the Octomaw goes on the attack. Swim laterally through your ink to avoid getting caught up in his incoming chomp attack. If you're not fast enough, you'll find yourself trapped in a cage made of the Octomaw's teeth. Throw a Splat Bomb at your feet to knock out most of the Octomaw's teeth, then step out of this lethal ring before you get chomped. When the Octomaw emerges from its ink, shoot out the remaining in the center of its mouth, then toss a Splat Bomb down its throat—aim for the black opening in the back of its mouth. If you hit the mark, the Octomaw's mouth gapes open, exposing a wiggling tentacle. Splat it with ink to end the first round.

Caution

If the Octomaw retreats to the perimeter of the platform following its initial attack, it will launch its remaining teeth at you. These teeth hover just above the platform, firing splotches of purple ink. You can avoid these attacks if you successfully toss a Splat Bomb down the Octomaw's throat or eliminate all of its teeth.

Round 2

In the second round, the platform is cleared of ink, making it tougher to move around. The Octomaw also moves much faster and its teeth are composed of a more durable metal. This makes his attacks more difficult to avoid and his teeth more resistant to your ink—it takes more hits to destroy each tooth. But the same tactics apply—escape his chomp attacks, shoot out his teeth, then toss a Splat Bomb down his throat. Follow this up by splatting the exposed tentacle.

Round 3

As the battle enters its final stage, the Octomaw's teeth are upgraded once again, replaced with sharp, gold chompers. It takes multiple hits to eliminate each tooth, so target one tooth at a time, particularly if you find yourself trapped in the Octomaw's open mouth. Remember, you don't have to destroy all the teeth—just the ones in the center blocking its throat. Once the center teeth are destroyed, lob a Splat Bomb down the Octomaw's throat to expose the tentacle one last time. After splatting the tentacle for the third time, the Octomaw explodes. Rush to the center of the platform and gather the Power Eggs and Sunken Scroll before rescuing the Zapfish.

Ink Battle Rewards

Weapon Unlock: New Squiffer

Visit Ammo Knights after retrieving the Sunken Scroll from the Ravenous Octomaw. Sheldon can use these blueprints to create the New Squiffer. You can purchase this new weapon for 4,500 gold and equip it during ink battles. You must reach level 11 before the weapon can be purchased.

amiibo Challenges

Defeating the Octomaw as part of an amiibo challenge provides Sheldon with blue prints he can use to manufacture new weapons. You can purchase these new weapons at Ammo Knights once you're level three or higher.

amiibo Gear Rewards			
Gear	Name	Cost	Required amiibo
	Hero Charger Replica	1,200	Inkling Girl
	Hero Roller Replica	1,200	Inkling Boy
	Hero Shot Replica	1,200	Inkling Squid

ZONE 5

Agents 1 and 2 are impressed by your performance. But Cap'n Cuttlefish is still missing, not to mention the Great Zapfish. It's still unclear who is behind this madness, but you're getting closer to uncovering the identity of the culprit. Still, the path ahead isn't easy. You must take the fight through six more lairs before you can board that suspicious-looking flying saucer orbiting Octo Valley.

Zone 5

Start

BB

23

22

25

24

26

27

Legend

22	Splat-Switch Revolution	**26**	Octoling Onslaught
23	Spongy Observatory	**27**	Unavoidable Flying Object
24	Pinwheel Power Plant	**BB**	Enter the Octobot King
25	Far-Flung Flooders		

SPLAT-SWITCH REVOLUTION

Splat-Switch Revolution

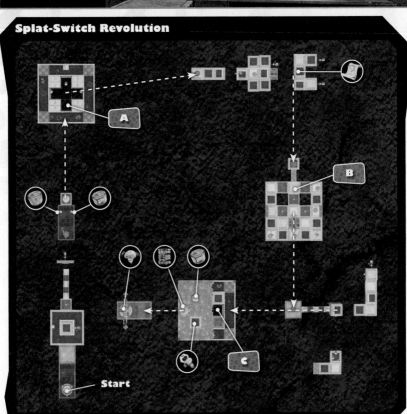

A

B

C

Start

Legend

	Key Locations			Armor
	Sunken Scroll			Inkzooka
	Key			Bubbler
	Vault			Bomb Rush
	Zapfish			Jump Path

A

Before leaping to this platform, choose the Bubbler special over the Inkzooka—you can only carry one special at a time, and Bubbler benefits you the most on this challenging platform. Initially you're attacked by three Octoballs. Lay a line of ink between you and the approaching Octoballs, but note that the glass portions of the platform cannot be inked. Once the Octoballs are eliminated, the glass sections rise, each topped with a Twintacle Octotrooper. Swim through your ink around the perimeter of the platform and pick off the Octotroopers one by one. If you haven't spread enough ink to swim, consider activating the Bubbler special.

Sunken Scroll

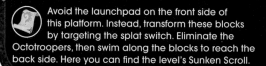

 Avoid the launchpad on the front side of this platform. Instead, transform these blocks by targeting the splat switch. Eliminate the Octotroopers, then swim along the blocks to reach the back side. Here you can find the level's Sunken Scroll.

 B

Before engaging the three Twintacle Octotroopers guarding this platform, take some time to spread some ink using Splat Bombs and Seekers. Swim through your ink to sneak up on the Octotroopers, taking them out one by one. But after eliminating the third Octotrooper, the platform transforms as two pillars rise, each occupied by one Octosniper. Immediately drop into your ink to avoid being spotted. Toss Splat Bombs or Seekers in attempt to divert their attention, then sneak up on each Octosniper and splat them at close range.

C

Upon landing here, spread some ink and engage the three Twintacle Octotroopers on the ground—grab the Bubbler special while you're at it. After eliminating the three Octotroopers, two Flooders arise from the floor and begin patrolling, joining a third Flooder topped by a vault and Octotrooper. The key to the vault is located on the floor where one of the Flooders emerged. Grab the key and immediately take the high ground, swimming up one of the two newly raised blocks. From here you can avoid the Flooders while targeting the Twintacle Octotrooper atop the vault. Hide in your ink until the Flooder approaches, then ambush the Octotrooper atop the vault. Opening the vault reveals the launchpad leading to the Zapfish.

Stage 23
SPONGY OBSERVATORY

Spongy Observatory

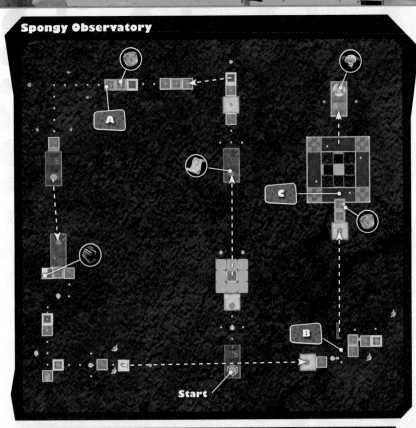

A

C

B

Start

Legend

	Key Locations		Armor
	Sunken Scroll		Inkzooka
	Key		Bubbler
	Vault		Bomb Rush
	Zapfish		Jump Path

Sunken Scroll

After crossing the second checkpoint, look over the edge—just below is a small platform. Swim down the nearby sponges to leap across to this platform. Smash the crate to retrieve the level's Sunken Scroll.

A

Use the Inkzooka provided here to rapidly eliminate the surrounding Octotroopers. Fire a tornado of ink across the line of sponges ahead to make them expand. Then cross the expanded sponges so you can hit the more distant Octotroopers. Eliminate these enemies as quickly as possible as their incoming blobs of ink will make the sponges shrink, potentially causing you to fall. Stay near the center of the sponges while firing the Inkzooka to avoid falling off—each shot fired knocks you backward.

B

These Octobombers are out of range of the nearby Balloon Fish, meaning you'll need to take them out directly. Stay hidden in your ink until you can swim close enough to each Octobomer to shoot them out of the sky. If you're detected, they'll continually toss Splat Bombs at you, potentially knocking you off the narrow platform or causing the sponge beneath your feet to shrink. So stay hidden until it's time to strike.

C

Two Octolings wait to ambush you on this final platform—but they only appear once you touch the platform. So ink all five sponges and spread more ink on the floor below before touching down on the platform. Standing atop the sponges gives you a good height advantage. But remember, if the sponges are hit by enemy ink, they'll shrink. So be ready to retreat to another sponge if you take heavy fire. If you find yourself on the floor, use the Inkzooka to blast tornados of ink at your Octoling foes. Once both Octolings are splatted, use the launchpad to reach the Zapfish.

Stage 24
PINWHEEL POWER PLANT

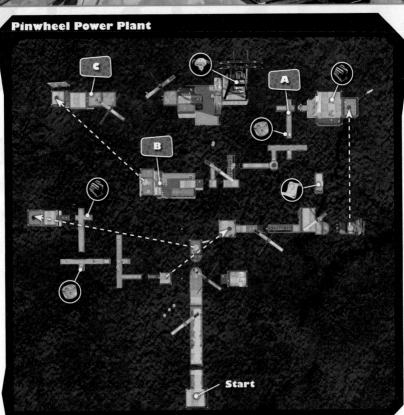

Pinwheel Power Plant

C

A

B

Start

Legend

	Key Locations		Armor
	Sunken Scroll		Inkzooka
	Key		Bubbler
	Vault		Bomb Rush
	Zapfish		Jump Path

Sunken Scroll

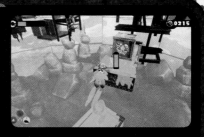

On the third platform, ink one of the blades of the second pinwheel and ride it until you can jump toward this platform—you'll need to enter squid form and swim before making this leap. The platform holds a crate containing the level's Sunken Scroll.

A Fight your way past an Octobomber and Octodiver here to reach this Inkzooka. Swim along the narrow path ahead, toward an Octocopter, until two Shielded Octotroopers appear on the neighboring platform ahead. Retreat to a safe distance and activate the Inkzooka, using it to take out these enemies. But watch your footing—each shot fired pushes you backward, potentially knocking you off this narrow walkway.

B This pinwheel is configured vertically, like a windmill. Stand on this elevated platform and ink as much of the pinwheel as possible. Ink the front face of the pinwheel as well as the inside surfaces of its two thick blades. When it's thoroughly inked, swim and then jump to the inked front face of the pinwheel. Transition to the inside portion of the blade and spread more ink if necessary before swimming through one of the nets. As the blade rotates to a vertical positon, swim up and jump onto the platform above. If you fall at any point, backtrack to the elevated platform, using a Gusher to quickly reach the top.

C In this section, you must traverse two moving horizontal platforms while avoiding two pinwheels. Eliminate the Octotrooper on the first pinwheel, then hop onto the moving platform—leap over the thick blade of the approaching pinwheel while swimming through its nets. Leap to the next moving platform and target the Octotrooper riding the pinwheel ahead. This time, jump onto one of the thick blades of the pinwheel and ride it around until you can safely drop onto the stationary platform ahead.

Stage 25
FAR-FLUNG FLOODERS

Far-Flung Flooders

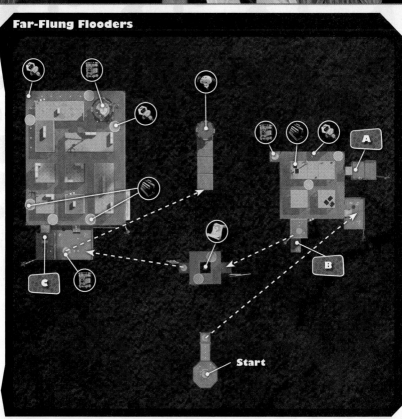

Start

Legend

	Key Locations		Armor
	Sunken Scroll		Inkzooka
	Key		Bubbler
	Vault		Bomb Rush
	Zapfish		Jump Path

98

A Use the ink spread by Seekers to sneak past the two Flooders on this platform to retrieve the key (on the right side) and open the vault—watch out for Octodivers hidden in the purple ink. The launchpad within the vault launches you to the platform's upper level. Here you come under attack by Twintacle Octotroopers riding atop the two Flooders. Hide in your ink and ambush the Octotroopers as they move into range.

B Bypass the launchpad on the upper level and drop down to this small platform to discover a hidden launchpad. If you want to collect the level's Sunken Scroll and some Power Eggs, use this launchpad to reach the platform in the center. The launchpad above completely bypasses this area, taking you directly to the final platform.

Sunken Scroll

The hidden launchpad leads to this platform occupied by two Flooders. The Sunken Scroll is located in the crate in the center. Activate the Gushers atop the Flooders to shoot the balloons high above the platform to collect some Power Eggs. Use the launchpad here to reach the final platform.

C There are six Flooders patrolling the lower portion of this platform. Veer left and use Seekers to paint narrow stripes of ink down these narrow corridors to reach the key. Return to the vault to access a Gusher providing access to the platform's upper level. An Octosniper has appeared on top of one of the Flooders—the other Flooders are topped by Octotroopers and crates containing armor. Hide in your ink and ambush the Octosniper and Octotroopers as they pass by. Use the key dropped by the Octosniper to open the vault at the back of the platform—this leads to the Zapfish.

Stage 26
OCTOLING ONSLAUGHT

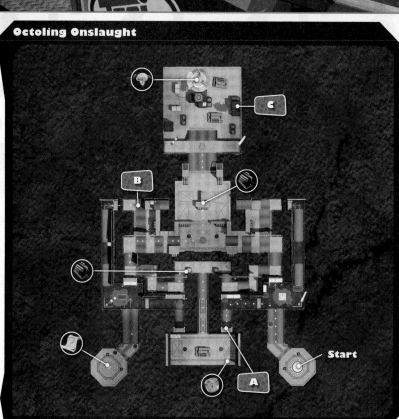

Octoling Onslaught

C

B

Start

A

Legend

	Key Locations			Armor
	Sunken Scroll			Inkzooka
	Key			Bubbler
	Vault			Bomb Rush
	Zapfish			Jump Path

If you've competed on Saltspray Rig during ink battles, this stage should look familiar. But there have been some alterations, making for a more linear progression. Before dropping down to this low area, pause at this ledge and wait for an Octoling to appear below. You'll have a much easier time splatting the Octoling from this elevated perch. Once the Octoling has been eliminated, drop down and grab the Inkzooka—this can come in handy later when you confront the Elite Octolings.

This Inkrail is the only way to reach the level's Sunken Scroll. But before activating and using the Inkrail, eliminate the Octolings in the immediate area, particularly those on the high ground. If you're struck by enemy ink while riding the Inkrail, you may fall into the water below. So eliminate all nearby threats before making a move for the Sunken Scroll.

Sunken Scroll

 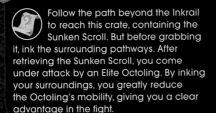 

Follow the path beyond the Inkrail to reach this crate, containing the Sunken Scroll. But before grabbing it, ink the surrounding pathways. After retrieving the Sunken Scroll, you come under attack by an Elite Octoling. By inking your surroundings, you greatly reduce the Octoling's mobility, giving you a clear advantage in the fight.

Upon entering this area, you come under attack by an Elite Octoling, indicated by the seaweed growing out of her head. Instead of going toe-to-toe with this challenging foe, ink the side of this tall stack of shipping containers and swim to the top. From this perch you can easily take out the Elite Octoling by spreading ink with your Hero Shot and Splat Bombs. Once the Elite Octoling is defeated, a second one attacks—hold this position to confront this threat. When the area is clear, use the Gusher to reach the Zapfish.

Stage 27
UNAVOIDABLE FLYING OBJECT

Unavoidable Flying Object

To Map Below

Start

A

B

C

From Map Above

Legend

Key Locations		Armor	
Sunken Scroll		Inkzooka	
Key		Bubbler	
Vault		Bomb Rush	
Zapfish		Jump Path	

Welcome back to Blackbelly Skatepark. This time the park is under attack by an Octostriker. Evade the incoming Inkstrikes and the Octosnipers while making an aggressive push to the top of this central tower. Grab the key and use the tower's height advantage to spread some ink onto the ground below—swim through this ink to hide from the Octosnipers. But don't linger here too long, or else you'll be hit with an Inkstrike.

Target the Balloon Fish in the pool section by the vault to rapidly coat the ground with ink. You'll need plenty of ink to swim through if you hope to sneak up on the two Octosnipers guarding the vault. Swim behind this bumper and toss a Splat Bomb between the two Octosnipers. Once the path is clear, open the vault with the key to reveal a launchpad. However, consider using the launchpad later, once you've recovered the Sunken Scroll.

Sunken Scroll

This dead-end corridor is guarded by an Octosniper. Once you've dealt with the Octosniper, swim up to this ledge to retrieve the Sunken Scroll.

Once you've reached the flying saucer, ink the perimeter and rush the Octostriker. But watch out for the Octobombers hovering above the flying saucer. Each Octobomber is positioned near a Balloon Fish. Instead of shooting the Octobombers, simply pop the Balloon Fish, spreading ink over a wide area and taking out these Splat Bomb-tossing foes. With the Octobombers under control, focus on the Octostriker—swim just beneath him, then shoot up with your Hero Shot. After the Octostriker has succumbed to your attacks, retrieve the Zapfish from the center of the flying saucer.

ENTER THE OCTOBOT KING

Enter the Octobot King

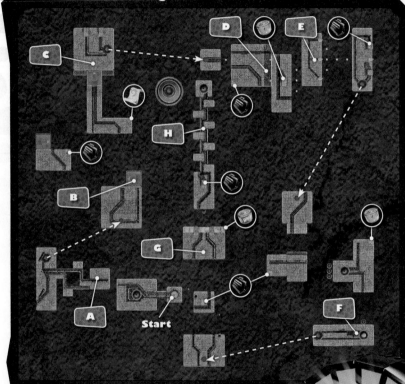

Legend

	Key Locations		Armor
	Sunken Scroll		Inkzooka
	Key		Bubbler
	Vault		Bomb Rush
	Zapfish		Jump Path

As you enter this boss's lair Cap'n Cuttlefish calls out, warning you that you're walking into a trap. But there's no turning back now. Within moments, the Octobot King, DJ Octavio, reveals himself—his hovering vehicle is powered by the Great Zapfish.

As DJ Octavio attacks, he fires a pair of Octorpedos in your direction—shoot them out of the air to spread friendly ink on the platform. DJ Octavio follows up the Octorpedo attack by launching the vehicle's fists at you—the right fist comes at you first, followed by the left. Repeatedly shoot the fists to send them flying back at DJ Octavio, knocking him back. If you get hit by one of these incoming fists, you'll get splatted, and forced to respawn at the previous checkpoint. So sidestep while shooting upward at these fists to avoid getting splatted.

Octorpedo

The Octorpedos fired by DJ Octavio explode on contact with any surface, spreading purple ink. However, if you shoot them in mid air, they'll explode, spreading your ink. So try to hit these projectiles while they're in flight. If you can't shoot them, sidestep or swim away from their point of impact. The speed of the Octorpedos increases as you progress through the battle, making them more difficult to target and dodge.

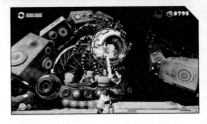

After knocking DJ Octavio back, pursue him across the platform. If you stay put, he'll just come charging back at you, and you'll make no progress in the battle. When DJ Octavio is backed up to the edge of the platform, he fires a massive squid-like missile in your direction. Like the incoming fist attacks, repeatedly shoot the approaching octomissile to send it flying back at DJ Octavio. But the boss uses the vehicle's fists to knock it back at you, so be ready to volley the octomissile back and forth. When the boss has no more fists to defend himself, the octomissile impacts, prompting DJ Octavio to retreat to a neighboring platform. Use the launchpad to follow him and resume your assault.

Octomissile

DJ Octavio only fires a octomissile when he has nowhere left to go. Shoot these large incoming missiles repeatedly to send them flying back at DJ Octavio. He'll respond by batting away the missile using his fist attacks. Keep volleying the missile back and forth until DJ Octavio has used both of his fist attacks. With no way to defend himself, the octomissile will impact, causing him to retreat.

Upon landing on the new platform, rush to the nearby Propeller Lift, but don't activate it just yet. DJ Octavio has a new attack, firing a lethal sonic attack called the Killer Wail—if you see this purple beam, get out of the way. Wait until the Killer Wail has been fired, then use the Propeller Lift to dodge DJ

Octavio's follow-up Octorpedo attacks—shoot the propeller on the lift to move laterally, making you a harder target to hit. While riding the Propeller Lift, keep shooting the incoming fist attacks to knock DJ Octavio back. Push forward and smash the crate on the next platform to retrieve some armor. Repel DJ Octavio's attacks again and board another Propeller Lift to keep pushing forward.

Sunken Scroll

 After using the second Propeller Lift, smash this crate to retrieve the level's Sunken Scroll. However, keep an eye on DJ Octavio. Don't make a move for the Sunken Scroll until there's a lull in attacks.

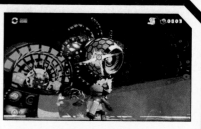

 Ride the next Propeller Lift to reach this platform. Dodge or counter DJ Octavio's attacks, pushing him farther and farther back to the edge of the platform. When he has nowhere left to run, DJ Octavio fires another octomissile. This is easy enough to repel—you need to knock it back three times

before it hits DJ Octavio. However, while targeting the octomissile, watch out for other incoming attacks. DJ Octavio continually fires Octorpedos at you as well as Killer Wails. So don't get caught focusing solely on the octomissile. Keep moving to avoid getting blindsided by these other attacks. Once DJ Octavio retreats, use the launchpad to follow him to the next platform.

Tip

Don't forget to stock up on armor during this fight. You can wear up to three pieces of armor at a time—each hit you take destroys one piece of armor, but prevents you from getting splatted. Armor is essential for surviving Killer Wail attacks, particularly when traversing narrow platforms that leave you little room to maneuver.

During this phase, DJ Octavio fires red balls, each containing an Octobomber or an Octocopter. Shoot these balls out of the sky before they land, otherwise you'll have to fight an Octobomber or Octocopter, making the advance even more challenging. Be careful when advancing across the

sponges on this platform. For best results, wait until DJ Octavio has been knocked back before swimming across the sponges. Otherwise they could get hit with enemy ink while you cross, causing them to shrink, potentially leading to a fatal fall.

Ball Attack

These incoming red balls contain different enemies. Shoot them out of the air to prevent them from hatching. Initially the balls contain Octobombers and Octocopters. But later you'll encounter Octoballs and Twintacle Octotroopers popping out of them.

 When you've pushed DJ Octavio back to this point, use the nearby Balloon Fish to your advantage. Not only do these spread ink and expand the adjacent sponges, but the explosions of ink all destroy (or knock back) incoming attacks, including the fist attacks. However,

you'll need to time it just right—if you explode the Balloon Fish too early, the attacks will come through, and you'll have a hard time seeing them due to all the friedly ink flying through the air. Once DJ Octavio has been pushed back, quickly advance across the sponges to reach the last platform in this section. Be ready to repel his octomissile attacks here—once again, the Balloon Fish can help you knock the missile back. Use the launchpad to keep up the chase once DJ Octavio retreats.

 These platforms are connected via invisible paths. Spread ink across these gaps to reveal these paths and keep applying pressure on DJ Octavio, pushing him farther and farther back—use the Gushers to ascend to the higher platforms. This time the red balls fired by DJ

Octavio contain Octoballs. So try to shoot these incoming balls out of the air to prevent complicating your already challenging advance. When DJ Octavio has nowhere left to go, knock back his octomissile to trigger his retreat. This time Agents 1 and 2 have succeeded in infiltrating the lair, pumping in the sweet sounds of the Squid Sisters. The music drives DJ Octavio mad, but it gives Cap'n Cuttlefish the strength to escape. It's time to make the final push—use the launchpad to follow DJ Octavio to the next platform.

During this phase, don't linger on the first two platforms very long—there's very little room to maneuver, making it difficult to dodge incoming attacks. As soon as you knock back DJ Octavio, use the Inkrails to advance to this wider platform. Here you have a better chance of sidestepping incoming attacks.

There's also a Bubbler in the nearby crate—this can come in handy as you make the final assault. The red balls DJ Octavio launches at you contain Twintacle Octotroopers. Shoot these balls out of the air to prevent these enemies from spawning.

 The final phase of the battle is extremely challenging, as there's very little room to maneuver on this narrow walkway. Stay near the center of the walkway, then sidestep to small perimeter platforms to avoid incoming Killer Wail attacks. Just be careful not to walk or swim off the ledge. If necessary, activate the Bubbler special to avoid getting splatted during this chaotic phase of the battle. Push DJ Octavio back toward the edge of this walkway until he launches his octomissile attack. One last time, volley the octomissile back and forth while continually watching out for Octorpedo and Killer Wail attacks. The battle is finally over once the

octomissile hits DJ Octavio—splat him as he comes flying out of his vehicle to declare victory.

Epilogue

Following the battle with DJ Octavio, the Great Zapfish is restored atop Inkopolis Tower—Callie and Marie report on its return, but have no idea where it was or how it was returned. But upon your return to Octo Valley, Cap'n Cuttlefish is more than happy to acknowledge your role in defeating the Octarians and rescuing the Great Zapfish.

DJ Octavio has been imprisoned in Octo Valley, not far from Cap'n Cuttlefish's watchful eye—he won't be bothering Inkopolis anytime soon.

Note

While talking to Cap'n Cuttlefish, a stone tablet ascends from the ground nearby. Interact with this tablet to view the game's credits. The credits are interactive—splat the screen with ink to reveal the names of the developers.

Ink Battle Rewards

Weapon Unlocks: Dynamo Roller and Gold Dynamo Roller

If you collected the Sunken Scroll during the battle with DJ Octavio, you can now purchase the Dynamo Roller (level 15, 10,000 gold) and Gold Dynamo Roller (level 20, 25,000 gold) from Sheldon at Ammo Knights. These rollers can be equipped and used during ink battles—they're ideal for spreading ink during Turf War matches.

Octo Valley Completion Rewards

After defeating DJ Octavio, you're awarded with the Hero Suit and Octosuit. Each suit consists of one piece of clothing, one pair of shoes, and one headgear item. These items appear in your inventory and can be equipped for use during ink battles.

Gear Rewards

Gear	Name	Rarity	Main Ability
	Hero Jacket Replica	★★	Swim Speed Up
	Hero Runners Replicas	★★	Quick Super Jump
	Hero Headset Replica	★★	Run Speed Up
	Octoling Armor Replica	★★	Ink Saver (Sub)
	Octoling Boots Replicas	★★	Special Saver
	Octoling Goggles Replica	★★	Bomb Range Up

amiibo Challenges

Defeating the Octobot King as part of an amiibo challenge unlocks new arcade games. You can play these on the arcade cabinet in the plaza or while waiting for an Ink battle match to start in the lobby.

amiibo Arcade Rewards

Game	Name	Required amiibo
	Squidball	Inkling Girl
	Squid Racer	Inkling Boy
	Squid Beatz	Inkling Squid

INK BATTLES

Whether you've rescued the Great Zapfish or not, ink battles are always available in Inkopolis. During these online four-on-four competitive matches your skills are put to the test, requiring quick reflexes as well as a sharp mind. Before you jump into your first match, take a moment to review the fundamentals of ink battles.

GETTING STARTED

Upon entering Inkopolis Tower, the following screen greets you, detailing your status while prompting you to join a battle. There's a wealth of information here, so let's take a closer look.

Level

This is your current level. You can level up by earning Battle Points, or BP. BP is awarded by participating in ink battles. The accompanying meter shows how much BP is required to reach your next rank. The level cap is twenty.

Rank

Starting with a rank of C-, win more ranked battles to increase your rank all the way to A+. But if you lose ranked battles, your rank can decrease. So keep winning to avoid losing progress. The number next to your rank shows how much rank experience you have—you need 100 rank experience to advance to the next rank.

Gold

As you earn BP, you also earn gold. There is a 1:1 relationship between BP and gold earned. So score as much BP as possible in a match to walk away with the same amount in gold. Gold can be used to purchase new weapons, clothing, shoes, and headgear.

Super Sea Snails

Super Sea Snails are only awarded during Splatfest events. Visit Spyke and use your Super Sea Snails to add sub ability slots to your gear. If your gear already has three sub ability slots, you can pay Spyke a Super Sea Snail to reroll all three sub abilities.

Vibe Meter

You gain and lose flags based on how many matches you win or lose, and this meter is reset each day. Winning a match always awards one flag. Losing a match will take away flags based on your current vibe. There are four ranks: Chill, Toasty, Smokin', and SO HAWT!! Visit Judd (in the Plaza) to receive a gold reward—the higher your vibe meter status, the more gold you'll receive.

Game Mode

Here you can see the current game mode: Turf War or Splat Zones. Press X to get a quick summary of the game mode's rules.

Stages

Here's a list of active stages. Press Y to enter one of the stages in Recon mode. This allows you to walk around the stage by yourself, ideal for exploring and strategizing before a battle.

Battle Selection

Here you can choose to participate in one of three different battle types: a regular battle, a ranked battle, or a regular battle with friends. If you want to play Turf War, choose a regular battle or regular battle with friends. If you want to play Splat Zones, choose ranked battle. Regardless of choice, you're immediately sent to a matchmaking screen where you're joined by teammates and opponents.

Ink Battle Interface

Once you've joined a match, you're thrust into an ink battle. Before you start inking territory and splatting opponents, take a moment to study these various on-screen elements.

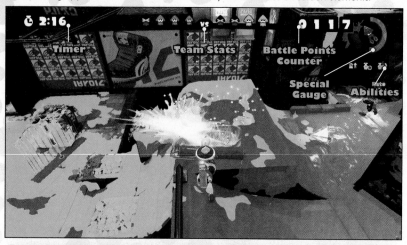

Timer

The timer shows how much time is remaining in the match. Turf War battles last a full three minutes. Splat Zones matches can last as long as five minutes, but can end early if victory conditions are met.

Team Status

Each squid icon represents a different player. Colored icons represent active players on the stage while grayed-out icons represent splatted players in the process of respawning. These icons change size based on a few factors:

- In Turf War, if it is a close match, both team's squid icons will be the same size. If one team is winning slightly, their Team Status icons become slightly larger. If one team is winning by a substantial margin, their Team Status icons get even larger and the losing team will have a "Danger!" icon appear.

- In ranked battles, if no one controls the objective, the squid icons are the same size. If one team controls the objective but isn't making progress towards a win, their Team Status icons become slightly larger. If one team controls the objective and is making progress towards a win, their Team Status icons become even larger and the opposing team will have a "Danger!" icon appear.

Battle Points Counter

This counter only appears in Turf War and indicates how much ground that you personally have covered in ink. At the end of the match, the amount of BP that you earn is this number plus a victory bonus of 300 if your team wins. For example, if you have covered 1,000 BP worth of ground and your team wins, you earn 1,300 BP. If your team does not win, you just earn this number in BP, with no bonus.

Special Gauge

The Special Gauge fills as you cover ground in your ink. Once it is full, the gauge will start sparkling and the "Press Right Stick" icon appears. Pressing the Right Stick activates your special. Once the special is activated, the gauge drains at a rapid pace, indicating how much time is left for your special. If you get splatted, you lose half the progress in your special gauge.

Abilities

These three icons represent the main abilities associated with your character's clothing, shoes, and headgear. Abilities affect your character in various ways. These icons light up when a sub ability is in use. Flip ahead to the Weapons and Gear chapter for more information on abilities.

GamePad: Turf Map and Super Jumps

Touch a teammate's icon on the Turf Map to launch your Inkling through the air, landing near the selected teammate.

While competing in ink battles, don't forget to look down at your GamePad from time to time. Here you can see the Turf Map. This map displays a live feed of ink coverage on the stage, allowing you to see where friendly and enemy ink is being spread. If you see a fresh patch of enemy ink appearing, you can determine where opponents are. The GamePad is also necessary to perform Super Jumps. Using the stylus, select a teammate (or friendly Squid Beacon) on the Turf Map to perform a Super Jump. This launches your character high into the air before landing next to your teammate—this is ideal for applying pressure on hotly contested areas of a stage. But exercise

caution when performing Super Jumps. Jumping to a teammate who is engaged in a heated battle can put you at a major disadvantage upon landing.

Caution

Unless you have the Stealth Jump ability equipped, opponents can see where you're going to land during a Super Jump—a ring-shaped icon appears on the spot where you're going to land. Sneaky opponents can use this info to ambush you.

Weapons

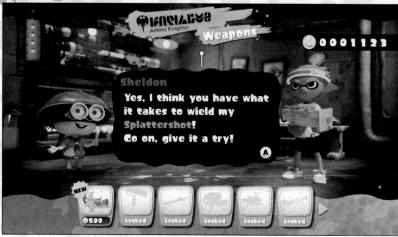

Sheldon is always excited to tell you about new weapons he has in stock at Ammo Knights. Level up to gain access to more weapons.

Initially, your Inkling comes equipped with the Splattershot Jr. main weapon, which includes the Splat Bomb sub weapon and Bubbler special—this is an excellent, versatile loadout for new players and veterans alike. As you level up, you can purchase new weapons from Sheldon at Ammo Knights. There are four different types of main weapons, each with their own strengths and weaknesses. Instead of purchasing every weapon that becomes available, focus on weapon types that best match your style of play. Here's a quick glimpse at the different types of weapons. For more information on weapons, sub weapons, and specials, reference the Weapons and Gear chapter.

Weapon Types

Weapon	Type	Description
	Rapid	Rapid-firing weapons are the most well-rounded, making them well-suited for spreading ink in Turf War or splatting opponents in any game mode.
	Charger	These weapons must be charged before firing to reach their high-damage, long-range. They're better suited for sniping opponents than for spreading ink.
	Roller	Rollers are ideal for rapidly spreading ink along flat, horizontal surfaces. They can also be swung to fling ink over wide areas or smack opponents.
	Blaster	These slow-firing, high-damage weapons fire ink-filled projectiles that explode in mid-air or upon impact. Their lack of range can make them difficult to use, but there's no denying their effectiveness in spreading ink.
	Sub Weapon	Each loadout comes equipped with a sub weapon, such as Splat Bombs. These weapons provide some welcome benefits, but they also consume a lot of ink.
	Special	Each loadout also includes a special, like Bubbler. Fill the special gauge by covering the stage with ink. Once the gauge is filled, you can activate the special.

Tip

Not sure which weapon to purchase? All weapons at Ammo Knights can be tested before you purchase them—press Y to enter the test phase. This allows you to experiment with the loadout's primary weapon, sub weapon, and special on a shooting range filled with various target dummies. The number above each target dummy reports how much damage it has taken from your attack. Testing before buying is a good idea in all instances.

Gear

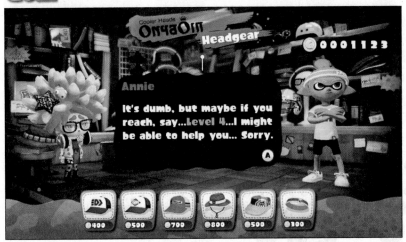

Annie: It's dumb, but maybe if you reach, say...Level 4...I might be able to help you... Sorry.

You need to reach level four before you can buy new clothing, shoes, or headgear.

The clothing, shoes, and headgear worn by your Inkling function like armor. Each piece of gear has a fixed main ability, which benefits your character in various ways. For example, the Damage Up ability increases the damage output of all your weapons. Since you have to wear clothing, shoes, and headgear at all times, you always have three main abilities active. Each piece of gear can also have up to three sub abilities. These lesser abilities aren't as effective, but since all abilities can be stacked, they work together to enhance the performance of your character during ink battles. New gear can be purchased with gold from Jelly Fresh, Shrimp Kicks, and Cooler Heads, located in the Plaza—check back regularly because their stock changes daily. For more information on abilities and gear, reference the Weapons and Gear chapter.

GAME MODES

There are two game modes available for online matches: Turf War and Splat Zones. In Turf War, it's all about covering the stage with as much ink as possible. But in ranked Splat Zones matches, both teams vie for control of one or two zones on the map, leading to some intense back-and-forth battles.

Turf War

When selecting a regular battle in the lobby, you're connected to a Turf War battle. In Turf War, each team struggles to ink as much of the stage as possible in their team's ink—only horizontal surfaces count. Whichever team has the most coverage at the end of the match wins, and BP is awarded based on two factors: the amount of ground you've covered and a 300 BP bonus if your team wins.

While splatting opponents is fun, don't lose sight of Turf War's primary objective—spreading ink.

Ranked Battles

The more matches you win, the quicker you rank up. You gain 20 rank experience with each win—each loss costs you 10 rank experience.

In ranked battles, your wins and losses are tracked across your career, determining your rank. All players begin with a rank of C-. But with continued wins, and accrued rank experience, you can climb the ranks, going up through C, C+, B-, B, B+, A-, A, and A+ ranks. You earn rank experience when you win a match. But if you lose a match, you lose rank experience, leading to a potential demotion in rank. You need 100 rank experience to advance to the next rank. Upon achieving a new rank, you're rewarded 30 rank experience, serving as a buffer, preventing you from getting demoted immediately if you suffer a loss. But if your rank experience dips below zero, you will fall down to the previous rank—you can't fall below a rank of C-.

Splat Zones

When selecting a ranked battle, you're connected to a Splat Zones match. The goal of Splat Zones is to control all Splat Zones (marked with yellow lines) by covering them in your team's ink. If your team covers a significant majority of the zone in their ink, the Splat Zone will become captured. If your team controls all Splat Zones (some stages have one Splat Zone and some stages have two Splat Zones), your team's score will begin counting down from 100 to 0. Splat Zone ownership is shown in between each team's score, under the Team Status. The objective of Splat Zones is to have your timer reach 0.

For best results, find an elevated perch near a Splat Zone and fire down on it from a safe distance.

If the trailing team captures all Splat Zones, the leading team incurs a time penalty based on how much further ahead they were—the further ahead, the harsher the penalty. This penalty is not taken into account in the final score. If neither team reaches 0, whichever team got the closest to 0 is the winner.

However, if the trailing team controls all Splat Zones when time runs out, the game goes into overtime until either the trailing team no longer controls all Splat Zones or the trailing team's score surpasses the leading team's score. At this point, the trailing team takes the lead and wins the match.

Note

Splat Zones isn't the only ranked game mode—expect more ranked battles in future software updates.

SPLATFEST

During Splatfest, night falls and the Plaza becomes very active. Miiverse posts show up in more places with greater frequency.

Splatfest is an event that happens occasionally where you get to vote for one of two teams to represent in a series of Turf War battles. Seven days before the Splatfest begins, during Inkopolis News, there's a special announcement that a Splatfest is coming. The theme of the Splatfest is announced, revealing the two teams you can vote for. After this announcement, a voting booth shows up next to the Miiverse posting box. At the voting booth you can vote for which team you want to represent during the Splatfest. Once you've chosen a team, you cannot change your vote. Twenty-four hours before the Splatfest starts, setup begins in the Plaza—some trucks arrive, indicating that Splatfest is about to begin. Once a Splatfest has begun, ranked and regular battles are unavailable— you can only participate in Splatfest battles.

Vote for your Splatfest team at this voting booth in the Plaza. You can vote as early as seven days before the Splatfest begins.

If you haven't chosen a team to represent in Splatfest, you will be unable to participate in online matches until you've chosen a team. Teams can be chosen at the voting booth at any time during Splatfest. Once you've chosen a team and entered the Splatfest lobby, instead of looking for eight players immediately, only four players will be required to queue for battle—specifically, four total players from the team that you've chosen.

Results and Rewards

Callie does her part to entertain the crowd during Splatfest.

Splatfest Titles and Rewards

Title	Total EXP Required	Super Sea Snails
Fanboy/Fangirl	—	2
Fiend	10	3
Defender	35	5
Champion	85	8
King/Queen	184	12

Splatfest EXP is earned by participating in and winning matches. Winning a match earns you three EXP, and your participation bonus is based on how much BP worth of ground you covered in ink during the match. If you cover 200–399 BP worth of ground, you earn one bonus participation EXP. If you cover 400 or more BP worth of ground, you earn two bonus participation EXP. Those are the only two thresholds for participation bonuses. So you can earn a maximum of five EXP per match if your team wins and you cover at least 400 BP worth of ground during the match.

Splatfest lasts for a few days. Once it's over, the results are announced during a broadcast of Inkopolis News. The results of a Splatfest are based on two factors:

• Popularity: The percentage of the vote each team got.

• Wins: The percentage of matches each team won—win percentage is worth double the value of popularity.

After the results, you're awarded Super Sea Snails based on the Splatfest Title you've earned. Super Sea Snails are used to add and reroll sub ability slots on gear via Spyke. If you're on the winning team, you'll earn double the Super Sea Snails— this means you can earn as many as twenty-four Super Sea Snails during Splatfest!

PLAZA ACTIVITIES

As addictive as ink battles are, don't forget to take a break and explore the Plaza. This is where you can spend some of your hard-earned gold on new weapons and gear. Visit Judd for gold bonuses or speak to Spyke to customize your gear.

Booyah Base

Booyah Base's three gear shops rotate their stock each day. But you'll need to level up before you can find new weapon selections at Ammo Knights.

Do you have gold burning a hole in your pocket? Then look no further than Booyah Base. This collection of shops is the perfect place to unload some gold in exchange for new weapons and gear. Visit Jelly Fresh, Shrimp Kicks, and Cooler Heads to purchase new clothing, shoes, and headgear. Stock is rotated daily in these shops, so check back frequently to see what new items the proprietors have for sale.

The weapon shop, Ammo Knights, is the odd one out since its stock is fixed and is based on your level. Each level that you gain allows access to at least one new weapon. In addition, you can earn the right to buy certain weapons from the shop by clearing amiibo challenges and defeating bosses in the game's single-player campaign. New weapons will be made available in the future with software updates, so don't forget to check back frequently.

JUDD: VIBE RANK BONUS

Speak to Judd to receive gold bonuses based on your vibe rank. Your vibe rank resets every day, so speak to Judd before ending your play session—otherwise you may be leaving bonus gold behind.

Vibe Rank and Rewards

Rank	Flags	Loss Penalty	Judd Reward
Chill	0	—	—
Toasty	1-3	-0.5 Flag	100 Gold
Smokin'	4-6	-1 Flag	300 Gold
SO HAWT!!	7+	-1.5 Flag	1,000 Gold

The more wins you string together, the more you ascend the vibe meter ranks, receiving a flag for each win. There are four ratings on the vibe meter, each determined by the number of flags you possess. However, you can lose flags too. Losing a match results in a penalty, potentially dropping your vibe rank.

So what's the point? Judd, the sleepy cat in the Plaza, will reward you with gold, giving different amounts based on your vibe rank—the higher the rank, the more gold you'll receive. These bonuses can only be claimed once per rank per day, and you will be awarded all unclaimed bonuses for previous ranks. For example, say on a Monday you reach Toasty rank and talk to Judd, who then awards you 100 bonus gold. Later on that same day, you reach Smokin' Rank and talk to Judd once again, and he will award you 300 additional bonus gold. On Tuesday, you reach Smokin' Rank again, but this time you did not talk to Judd while you were Toasty rank. When you go talk to Judd, he will award you 400 bonus gold: 100 for Toasty and 300 for Smokin'—this bonus is awarded all at once and isn't shown as a separate 100 and 300 bonus. So make a habit of speaking to Judd at least once per day, preferably at the end of your play session.

SPYKE: ORDERS AND SUB ABILITIES

See somefing you fancy, love?

Snorkel	Varsity Jacket	LE Lo-Tops
Order	Order	Order

Open Orders

Can't find the clothing, shoes, or headgear you want in the stores? Inspect the gear of fellow Inklings in the Plaza and ask Spyke to order you the same items.

Visit Spyke in the Plaza's alley once you've reached level four or higher—Spyke doesn't do business with newbies. Spyke offers two options: Orders and Slots. To obtain an order from Spyke, you must first place an order by interacting with one of the Inklings in the Plaza. If you see a piece of gear an Inkling has that you want, you can order an exact replica of the clothing, shoes, or headgear from Spyke—select the Order Gear option, then choose the gear you wish to order. YThe gear you select for your order will be an exact replica, with the same sub abilities. Or if you prefer, you can order a stripped-down version of the gear, with no unlocked sub abilities. You can place up to three orders at a time. However, the gear Spyke delivers the next day is randomized among your placed orders. So if you really want

a piece of gear, only place one order at a time to avoid delays in delivery. Spkye cannot order gear unlocked by completing the single-player campaign or amiibo challenges-you must earns those items on your own.

If you're not happy with the sub abilities associated with your clothing, shoes, or headgear, Spyke can help you out.

The gear you select for your order will be an exact replica, with the same sub abilities. Or if you prefer, you can order a stripped-down version of the gear, with no unlocked sub abilities. You can place up to three orders at a time. However, the gear Spyke delivers the next day is randomized among your placed orders. So if you really want a piece of gear, only place one order at a time to avoid delays in delivery. Spkye cannot order gear unlocked by completing the single-player campaign or amiibo challenges-you must earns those items on your own.

Spyke can also reroll the sub abilities associated with your clothing, shoes, and headgear for the price of one Super Sea Snail—choose the Slots option, then select the piece of gear you wish to reroll. Once confirmed, all the slots on the piece of gear you've selected are randomized. Rerolling sub abilities makes sense when you're unsatisfied with their current configuration. For more information on abilities and sub abilities, view the Abilities section in the Weapons and Gear chapter.

Note

If you're completely out of Super Sea Snails, Spyke will sell you one for 30,000 gold. But you must be level 20 before he'll sell you one of his own Super Sea Snails.

121

WEAPONS & GEAR

WEAPONS

As you level up, check back with Sheldon at Ammo Knights to see what weapons are available for purchase.

The more you participate in ink battles, the quicker you level up. With each level you obtain, you unlock weapons available for purchase at Ammo Knights—speak with Sheldon and he'll be more than happy to tell you all about the new weapons he has in stock. Each weapon is unique, with varied ranges, rates of fire, and damage output. Before spending your hard-earned gold, give each weapon a quick test drive to ensure it matches your ink battle needs and style of play. Sheldon allows weapons to be tested on a shooting range before you purchase them. Pay attention to the weapon's loadout too. Each weapon has its own sub weapon and special. Take into account how all three weapons work together. Some loadouts are better suited for Turf War, while others may work better in Splat Zones. If you don't care for a certain weapon, set it aside and save your money for future unlocks. Purchased weapons can be equipped immediately, ready for your next ink battle.

Note

New weapons are also unlocked by gathering the Sunken Scrolls left behind by the bosses in Octo Valley. These Sunken Scrolls are blueprints that Sheldon can use to craft new weapons. But before a weapon can be crafted, you must reach a certain level, as shown in the following table.

Weapon Unlock Progression

Weapon	Level Unlocked	Cost	Sub Weapon	Special	Single-Player Requirement
Splattershot Jr.	1	—	Splat Bomb	Bubbler	—
Splattershot	2	500	Burst Bomb	Bomb Rush	—
Custom Splattershot Jr.	2	800	Disruptor	Echolocator	Requires Octostomp Sunken Scroll
Splat Roller	3	1,000	Suction Bomb	Killer Wail	—
Splat Charger	3	1,000	Splat Bomb	Bomb Rush	—
Tentatek Splattershot	4	2,000	Suction Bomb	Inkzooka	—
Kelp Splat Charger	4	2,500	Sprinkler	Killer Wail	Requires Octonozzle Sunken Scroll
.52 Gal	5	3,000	Splash Wall	Killer Wail	—
Classic Squiffer	6	5,000	Point Sensor	Bubbler	—
Krak-On Splat Roller	7	3,000	Squid Beakon	Kraken	—
Aerospray MG	7	4,500	Seeker	Inkzooka	Requires Octowhirl Sunken Scroll
Jet Squelcher	8	4,000	Splash Wall	Inkstrike	—
Blaster	9	3,500	Disruptor	Killer Wail	—
Splattershot Pro	10	8,000	Splat Bomb	Inkstrike	—
.52 Gal Deco	11	4,500	Seeker	Inkstrike	—
New Squiffer	11	4,500	Ink Mine	Inkzooka	Requires Octomaw Sunken Scroll
.96 Gal	12	7,600	Sprinkler	Echolocator	—
Splatterscope	13	3,500	Splat Bomb	Bomb Rush	—
Aerospray RG	13	16,800	Ink Mine	Inkstrike	Requires Octowhirl Sunken Scroll
Rapid Blaster	14	10,000	Ink Mine	Bubbler	—
Custom Jet Squelcher	15	7,900	Burst Bomb	Kraken	—
Dynamo Roller	15	7,900	Sprinkler	Echolocator	Requires Octobot King Sunken Scroll
Dual Squelcher	16	9,800	Splat Bomb	Echolocator	—
Custom Blaster	17	6,800	Point Sensor	Bubbler	—
Kelp Splatterscope	17	7,800	Sprinkler	Killer Wail	—
E-Liter 3K	18	12,500	Burst Bomb	Echolocator	—
Rapid Blaster Deco	19	14,800	Suction Bomb	Bomb Rush	—
Forge Splattershot Pro	20	19,800	Point Sensor	Inkzooka	—
Gold Dynamo Roller	20	25,000	Splat Bomb	Inkstrike	Requires Octobot King Sunken Scroll

Splattershot Jr.

Weapon Stats:

Range		32
Damage		32
Fire Rate		75

Sub Weapon:
Splat Bomb

Special:
Bubbler

Description:

Everyone's got to start somewhere. Good rate of fire and efficient ink use to boot. Not the most accurate of weapons, but it sprays ink so wildly you're bound to hit something.

Weapon Type:	Rapid
Level Unlocked:	1
Cost:	0
Base Damage:	28

Notes:

The Splattershot Jr. excels at turf coverage, making it an apt choice for Turf Wars. Bubbler allows this loadout to be a good support option since you can share Bubbler with nearby teammates. Splat Bombs, on the other hand, can be used to set clever traps or keep enemies at a distance. Even though it's the starting weapon, few loadouts are as versatile as this one. This makes it a good choice when learning new stages and game modes.

Splattershot

Weapon Stats:

Range		50
Damage		45
Fire Rate		55

Sub Weapon:
Burst Bomb

Special:
Bomb Rush

Description:

Developed after the Great Turf War, this weapon is easy enough for anyone to use. A great all-arounder with few weak points. A trusty companion through thick and thin.

Weapon Type:	Rapid
Level Unlocked:	2
Cost:	500
Base Damage:	36

Notes:

This loadout is great for Turf War thanks to the coverage ability of the Burst Bombs and the Bomb Rush special. Ink Saver (Main) and Bomb Range Up are abilities you should consider for this weapon loadout. The weapon itself is the strength of this loadout, and Ink Saver (Main) allows you to fire more shots, making up for its coverage ability. Bomb Range Up helps you throw those Burst Bombs farther, thus covering more ground at a greater distance.

Custom Splattershot Jr.

Weapon Stats:

Range		32
Damage		32
Fire Rate		75

Sub Weapon:
Disruptor

Special:
Echolocator

Description:
A new build of the Splattershot Jr., built by Sheldon after being inspired by some odd fluid he found stuck to the blueprints. Throw Disruptors at your opponents to slow them down.

Weapon Type: Rapid
Level Unlocked: 2
(Requires Octostomp Sunken Scroll)
Cost: 800
Base Damage: 28

Notes:
The Custom Splattershot Jr. is an all-around team support weapon. Disruptor might give the weapon enough utility to lose Ninja Squid and replace it with Ink Saver Sub or Special Charge Up—but those abilities should only be considered for someone who's willing to sit back and accept a pure support role over a hybrid one.

Splat Roller

Weapon Stats:

Range		55
Ink Speed		50
Handling		40

Sub Weapon:
Suction Bomb

Special:
Killer Wail

Description:
A weapon adapted from an ordinary paint roller. Aside from inking the ground, it can also be swung to hurl globs of ink at your opponents.

Weapon Type: Roller
Level Unlocked: 3

Cost: 1,000
Splash Damage: 25-125
Roll Damage: 140

Notes:
This basic roller has decent ink splatter range and roll speed. The Suction Bomb can be used to force opponents away from a specific spot, which may put them in range of a melee strike—or you can simply roll over them as they attempt to escape the Suction Bomb's blast.

Splat Charger

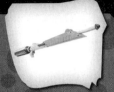

Weapon Stats:

Range		85
Charge Speed		50
Mobility		40

Sub Weapon:
Splat Bomb

Special:
Bomb Rush

Description:
Charges up before releasing a concentrated, high-powered burst with excellent range. Charging takes a while, so be careful not to open yourself up to attack!

Weapon Type: Charger
Level Unlocked: 3

Cost: 1,000
No Charge Damage: 40
Full Charge Damage: 140

Notes:
In terms of stats, the Splat Charger sits right in the middle of the chargers, and thus has the most versatility and the possibility to adjust for play style. Splat Bombs are powerful tools on their own from mid-range, so Ink Saver (Sub) and Bomb Range Up can be particularly useful abilities when using this loadout.

Tentatek Splattershot

Weapon Stats:

Range		50
Damage		45
Fire Rate		55

Sub Weapon:
Suction Bomb

Special:
Inkzooka

Description:
A slick Splattershot developed in collaboration with top gear brand Tentatek. With all-new options, the Tentatek Splattershot ensures you'll be ready for anything.

Weapon Type: Rapid
Level Unlocked: 4

Cost: 2,000
Base Damage: 36

Notes:
This loadout is most useful during ranked Splat Zones matches. Suction Bombs can be used to set traps behind walls in Splat Zones. The Inkzooka allows you to put up a fight from a much greater distance and hit enemies who are on higher ground. Ink Saver (Main) and Ink Saver (Sub) are abilities you should consider when equipping this loadout.

Kelp Splat Charger

Weapon Stats:

Range		85
Charge Speed		50
Mobility		40

Sub Weapon:
Sprinkler

Special:
Killer Wail

Description:

A Splat Charger modified by Sheldon using some seaweed that was stuck to the blueprints. Maybe the Sprinkler sub weapon is meant to keep the seaweed fresh?

Weapon Type: Charger

Level Unlocked: 4
(Requires Octonozzle Sunken Scroll)

Cost: 2,500

No Charge Damage: 40

Full Charge Damage: 160

Notes:

Statistically, this weapon is nearly identical to the Splat Charger. But the Sprinkler/Killer Wail duo promote a more reserved approach. The Killer Wail special is very powerful when aimed down narrow corridors. Consider using the Special Charge Up ability to use Killer Wail with greater frequency.

.52 Gal

Weapon Stats:

Range		50
Damage		70
Fire Rate		30

Sub Weapon:
Splash Wall

Special:
Killer Wail

Description:

A high-powered weapon that pumps out a lot of ink with each shot. It doesn't take many shots to splat an opponent, which is a good thing given its rather slow rate of fire.

Weapon Type: Rapid

Level Unlocked: 5

Cost: 3,000

Base Damage: 52

Notes:

The .52 Gal excels at offensive game modes like Splat Zones—it only takes two shots from this weapon to splat opponents, making it a great choice for offensively minded players. Consider using a Damage Up ability in place of Ink Saver to help break an enemy's Defense Up buff, or use Special Charge Up to compensate for the weapon's low rate of fire.

Classic Squiffer

Weapon Stats:

Range		65
Charge Speed		70
Mobility		60

Sub Weapon:
Point Sensor

Special:
Bubbler

Description:

A charger equipped with a miniaturized ink compression tank. The charge time is short, but it still packs a serious punch. The range leaves a little to be desired.

Weapon Type:	Charger
Level Unlocked:	6
Cost:	5,000
No Charge Damage:	40
Full Charge Damage:	140

Notes:

A relatively short-ranged charger, the Classic Squiffer's quick charge time and high damage make it a formidable weapon in the right hands. This is great for engaging enemies directly and harassing objectives. While you can use the Bubbler to extricate yourself from tight spots, the Defense Up ability is recommended for additional safety during hit-and-run attacks.

Krak-On Splat Roller

Weapon Stats:

Range		55
Ink Speed		50
Handling		40

Sub Weapon:
Squid Beakon

Special:
Kraken

Description:

Created in association with Krak-On, the freshest name in footwear. The sub weapon allows you to create a Super Jump point for your team, and the special lets you surge across the battlefield.

Weapon Type:	Roller
Level Unlocked:	7
Cost:	3,000
Splash Damage:	25-125
Roll Damage:	140

Notes:

This is a variation of the Splat Roller. Squid Beakon can be used for support to offer some Super Jump points to help your team. The Kraken is a very strong offensive special, especially useful during Splat Zones—capturing a zone as an invincible Kraken is relatively easy.

Aerospray MG

Weapon Stats:

Range	32
Damage	20
Fire Rate	100

Sub Weapon:
Seeker

Special:
Inkzooka

Description:

Created by Sheldon from his grandfather's blueprints. Extremely high rate of fire. Each shot is weak individually, but a sustained barrage can really pressure opponents.

Notes:

The Aerospray MG covers a lot of ground quickly, making it great for Turf War—but serviceable at best in Splat Zones. This is primarily a short-range weapon—use the Inkzooka special for long-range engagements. Use the Ink Saver ability to reduce the amount of ink this weapon consumes. This allows you to use a Seeker to find and defeat enemy players while continually shooting, covering more ground and capturing Splat Zones.

Weapon Type: Rapid
Level Unlocked: 7
(Requires Octowhirl Sunken Scroll)
Cost: 4,500
Base Damage: 24.5

Jet Squelcher

Weapon Stats:

Range	80
Damage	32
Fire Rate	40

Sub Weapon:
Splash Wall

Special:
Inkstrike

Description:

Designed to maximize range in order to effectively take on charger-type weapons. Boasts the greatest range of any automatic ink shooter.

Notes:

The Jet Squelcher's long-range capability is its greatest strength. This weapon allows you engage distant targets without using a charger. With Splash Wall and Inkstrike, this allows you to stay far away from the action and still make meaningful contributions to battles. Splash Wall can be used to trap people in corridors or block ramps to key areas. Consider using the Ink Saver (Main) ability, as only one Splash Wall can be deployed at a time.

Weapon Type: Rapid
Level Unlocked: 8

Cost: 4,000
Base Damage: 31

Blaster

Weapon Stats:

Range		25
Impact		70
Fire Rate		20

 Sub Weapon:
Disruptor

 Special:
Killer Wail

Description:
Fires a special ink shot that explodes in mid-air. This explosion can be used to attack a wide area.

Weapon Type: Blaster
Level Unlocked: 9

Cost: 3,500
No Charge Damage: 50
Full Charge Damage: 125

Notes:
This weapon fires grenade-like munitions that spread ink over a wide area.The large area of effect on its blast is its core strength, allowing you to ink around corners and splat players who are trying to take cover. Despite its low rate of fire, the Blaster consumes ink quickly. Consider using the Ink Saver (Main) ability to keep your ink tank from running dry.

Splattershot Pro

Weapon Stats:

Range		68
Damage		55
Fire Rate		40

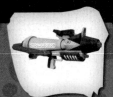

 Sub Weapon:
Splat Bomb

Special:
Inkstrike

Description:
An updated Splattershot developed with advanced battles in mind. Consumes a lot of ink and has a slow rate of fire, but its range and accuracy are vastly improved.

Weapon Type: Rapid
Level Unlocked: 10

Cost: 8,000
Base Damage: 42

Notes:
Thanks to its high damage output and long range, the Splattershot Pro is great for engaging opponents, but less effective at spreading ink. This makes it well-suited for Splat Zones matches. Consider using Ink Saver (Sub) for this one—it'll leave you more ink after using a Splat Bomb so you can continue your assault. Use Splat Bombs to force enemies out of hiding, then splat them with your primary weapon.

.52 Gal Deco

Weapon Stats:

Range		50
Damage		70
Fire Rate		30

Sub Weapon:
Seeker

Special:
Inkstrike

Description:
A bedazzled .52 Gal shooter. Your opponents may laugh at you. . .until you run them down with Seekers and the almighty Inkstrike.

Notes:
Same as the .52 Gal, but the loadout grants you more mobility with Seekers and greater offensive capability with Inkstrike. This loadout is great for Splat Zones—use Inkstrike from a distance to contest Splat Zones. Use the Special Charge Up ability in place of Run Speed Up, as Seekers already give the .52 Gal Deco plenty of room to navigate a stage quickly.

Weapon Type: Rapid
Level Unlocked: 11

Cost: 4,500
Base Damage: 52

New Squiffer

Weapon Stats:

Range		65
Charge Speed		70
Mobility		60

Sub Weapon:
Ink Mine

Special:
Inkzooka

Description:
Sheldon has used the blueprints to adjust the sub and special setup. Trap your opponents in a sticky situation with the sub, or deliver a long-range strike with the special.

Notes:
While this weapon shares the upsides and downsides of the Classic Squiffer, the addition of Ink Mines, in particular, adds effectiveness to hit-and-run attacks and objective control. With no Bubbler to keep you safe, consider using the Defense Up ability so you can absorb more damage.

Weapon Type: Charger
Level Unlocked: 11
(Requires Octomaw Sunken Scroll)
Cost: 4,500
No Charge Damage: 40
Full Charge Damage: 140

.96 Gal

Weapon Stats:

Range		68
Damage		80
Fire Rate		15

Sub Weapon:
Sprinkler

Special:
Echolocator

Description:

Similar to the .52 Gal, but with an improved mechanism and a more stable shot. Range and power have been increased . . . at the cost of being even more ink hungry.

Weapon Type:	Rapid
Level Unlocked:	12
Cost:	7,600
Base Damage:	62

Notes:

This weapon's slow fire rate and high ink consumption makes it a poor choice for Turf War. But its range and power make up for its lack of coverage in Splat Zones. Since you can only have one Sprinkler on the field at a time, consider using the Ink Saver (Main) ability over Ink Saver (Sub). This will let you make the most of what ink you have left after using a Sprinkler.

Splatterscope

Weapon Stats:

Range		88
Charge Speed		50
Mobility		35

Sub Weapon:
Splat Bomb

Special:
Bomb Rush

Description:

A Splat Charger fitted with a scope to allow for precision aiming. The range has been increased, but the field of vision is rather narrow.

Weapon Type:	Charger
Level Unlocked:	13
Cost:	3,500
No Charge Damage:	40
Full Charge Damage:	160

Notes:

The Splatterscope is identical to the Splat Charger, but is equipped with a scope for slightly greater long-range precision. To avoid getting blindsided, only peer through the scope prior to firing. If you find yourself under attack at close range, use the Bomb Rush special to make your escape, tossing Splat Bombs to put some distance between yourself and your attackers.

Aerospray RG

Weapon Stats:

Range		32
Damage		20
Fire Rate		100

Sub Weapon:
Ink Mine

Special:
Inkstrike

Description:
An Aerospray MG with variant sub and special weapons, courtesy of Sheldon. Give foes a nasty surprise with Ink Mines, or drop an Inkstrike on them when they least expect it.

Notes:
This weapon performs similarly to the Aerospray MG, but the loadout comes with Ink Mine instead of the Seeker. This loadout is more effective in Splat Zones than Turf War. Consider using the Ink Recovery Up ability to replenish ink faster after dropping an Ink Mine near an objective or chokepoint.

Weapon Type: Rapid
Level Unlocked: 13
(Requires Octowhirl Sunken Scroll)
Cost: 16,800
Base Damage: 24.5

Rapid Blaster

Weapon Stats:

Range		45
Impact		35
Fire Rate		40

Sub Weapon:
Ink Mine

Special:
Bubbler

Description:
Mitigates the weaknesses of the regular Blaster by giving up a little shot power for a better rate of fire.

Notes:
It takes two hits from the Rapid Blaster to splat your opponents, but you'll need to get in close to score direct hits. Bubbler is essential for surviving these close-quarter encounters. Special Charge Up, Special Duration Up, and the Special Saver abilities let you activate Bubbler with greater frequency.

Weapon Type: Blaster
Level Unlocked: 14
Cost: 10,000
Min. Splash Damage: 25
Direct Hit Damage: 80

Custom Jet Squelcher

Weapon Stats:

Range		80
Damage		32
Fire Rate		40

Sub Weapon:
Burst Bomb

Special:
Kraken

Description:
A customized Jet Squelcher. The sub weapon lets you corner your opponents, and the quirky special weapon makes for a tricky package.

Weapon Type: Rapid
Level Unlocked: 15

Cost: 7,900
Base Damage: 31

Notes:
The Custom Jet Squelcher shares the same strengths as its squelcher brethren. Burst Bombs help with turf coverage, and Kraken gives you an offensive or defensive out for any situation. Consider using the Special Charge Up and Special Duration Up abilities with this loadout. This will help you unleash the Kraken more frequently, and do so for a longer period of time.

Dynamo Roller

Weapon Stats:

Range		72
Ink Speed		30
Handling		20

Sub Weapon:
Sprinkler

Special:
Echolocator

Description:
Using the blueprints as a starting point, Sheldon rigged up a motor to the roller base. Cumbersome to use, but delivers a powerful burst of ink when swung.

Weapon Type: Roller
Level Unlocked: 15
(Requires Octobot King Sunken Scroll)
Cost: 7,900
Splash Damage: 25-125
Roll Damage: 160

Notes:
The Dynamo Roller has a low swing speed and roll speed, but a higher damage output and ink splatter range. This roller is very useful when you have a height advantage over your opponents, standing over a Splat Zone for example. Just raining ink down with your swing can easily capture the zone. The Sprinkler can be used as a distraction for opponents, and Echolocator helps you keep tabs on your opponents so you're not snuck up on—which can be bad due to the slow attack speed of a Dynamo Roller.

Dual Squelcher

Weapon Stats:

Range		68
Damage		27
Fire Rate		55

Sub Weapon:
Splat Bomb

Special:
Echolocator

Description:
A double-barreled Jet Squelcher with a much higher rate of fire. The power of each shot is low, but the ample range and firing rate make up for it.

Weapon Type: Rapid
Level Unlocked: 16

Cost: 9,800
Base Damage: 28

Notes:
Compared to the Jet Squelcher, the Dual Squelcher has a little less range, but makes up for it with a slightly faster fire rate. The Dual Squelcher comes with Splat Bombs and Echolocator. This is really nice for supporting your teammates and giving them cover fire. Selecting the Ink Saver (Sub) ability over Ink Saver (Main) is best due to the amount of ink the Splat Bomb needs. Another ability to strive for is Bomb Range Up, so you can throw those Splat Bombs at a greater distance, eschewing the need to get close to your opponents.

Custom Blaster

Weapon Stats:

Range		25
Impact		70
Fire Rate		20

Sub Weapon:
Point Sensor

Special:
Bubbler

Description:
A customized Blaster. The sub weapon lets you track down your opponents so you can take them down with the wide-range Blaster shot.

Weapon Type: Blaster
Level Unlocked: 17
Direct Hit Damage: 125
Cost: 6,800
Min. Splash Damage: 50

Notes:
This powerful weapon can splat opponents with one direct hit. The Bubbler special makes the weapon's one-hit-kill capability even more dangerous for your opponents. Equip the Special Charge Up, Special Duration Up, and Special Saver abilities to utilize Bubbler with greater frequency and for longer durations.

Kelp Splatterscope

Weapon Stats:

Range		88
Charge Speed		50
Mobility		35

Sub Weapon:
Sprinkler

Special:
Killer Wail

Description:
A Splatterscope Sheldon modified in the same way as the Kelp Splat Charger—by sticking seaweed to it. Naturally, it also has a Sprinkler.

Weapon Type: Charger

Level Unlocked: 17

Cost: 7,800

No Charge Damage: 40

Full Charge Damage: 160

Notes:
The Kelp Splatterscope has the same stats the Kelp Splat Charger. The addition of a scope allows for greater precision when engaging targets at close range. But don't get tunnel vision. Identify targets in the third-person view before peering through the scope to take a shot. If you spend too much time peering through the magnified scope, you're likely to be flanked and splatted from behind.

E-Liter 3K

Weapon Stats:

Range		97
Charge Speed		20
Mobility		15

Sub Weapon:
Burst Bomb

Special:
Echolocator

Description:
A charger with a high-capacity tank. By packing a lot of ink into each shot, it can strike from a great distance . . . at the cost of long charge time and ferocious ink consumption.

Weapon Type: Charger

Level Unlocked: 18

Cost: 12,500

No Charge Damage: 40

Full Charge Damage: 180

Notes:
The longest-ranged weapon in the game, and thus truly terrifying on stages that allow sniping from afar. The Echolocator special helps with picking off unwary enemies and avoiding attackers from behind. The weapon suffers when engaging at close range, however, so abilities that emphasize mobility (like Run Speed Up and Swim Speed Up) are recommended.

Rapid Blaster Deco

Weapon Stats:

Range		45
Impact		35
Fire Rate		40

Sub Weapon:
Suction Bomb

Special:
Bomb Rush

Description:
A decorated version of the Rapid Blaster. Its sub weapon can scatter opponents, and its special lets you maximize that potential. A great set for staving off aggressive foes.

Weapon Type: Blaster
Level Unlocked: 19

Cost: 14,800
Min. Splash Damage: 25
Direct Hit Damage: 80

Notes:
This weapon has lower damage output and impact size than most of the other blasters. But the combination of Suction Bombs and Bomb Rush presents some enticing offensive and defensive opportunities, allowing you to scatter these explosive devices over a wide area. Equip the Ink Saver (Sub) and Defense Up abilities and use Suction Bombs to keep opponents away from you.

Forge Splattershot Pro

Weapon Stats:

Range		68
Damage		55
Fire Rate		40

Sub Weapon:
Point Sensor

Special:
Inkzooka

Description:
A Splattershot Pro created in partnership with Forge, the only name in high-quality sports gear. A tricky Point Sensor sub weapon supports the reliable main weapon.

Weapon Type: Rapid
Level Unlocked: 20

Cost: 19,800
Base Damage: 42

Notes:
This weapon is lethal from a distance and great for competitive play. But it shoots very straight and is outclassed by other weapons in terms of turf coverage. This is a three-hit-kill weapon, but its low rate of fire can leave you at a disadvantage when facing opponents with faster firing weapons, like the Splattershot Jr. That said, keeping your foe at a distance is key here—consider the Ink Saver (Main) ability if you trust your aim, and Ink Saver (Sub) if your faith waivers.

Gold Dynamo Roller

Weapon Stats:

Range		72
Ink Speed		30
Handling		20

Sub Weapon:
Splat Bomb

Special:
Inkstrike

Description:
A Dynamo Roller with rearranged sub and special weapons. Lure the enemy out of hiding with the sub weapon, and then unleash the full force of your powerful roller.

Weapon Type: Roller
Level Unlocked: 20
(Requires Octobot King Sunken Scroll)
Cost: 25,000
Splash Damage: 25-125
Roll Damage: 160

Notes:
This is a well-rounded loadout, ideal for ink coverage and offensive pushes. Splat Bombs offer additional ranged damage, helping scatter opponents and forcing them where you want them. Inkstrike gives the loadout even more offensive range, great for contesting Splat Zones without putting yourself at risk.

amiibo WEAPONS

If you happen to own the Inkling Boy, Inkling Girl, or Squid amiibo, you can unlock more weapons by completing amiibo challenges. Unlocking these weapons requires you to defeat the Octomaw boss.

Hero Shot Replica

Weapon Stats:

Range		50
Damage		45
Fire Rate		55

Sub Weapon:
Burst Bomb

Special:
Bomb Rush

Description:
A sweet replica created by Sheldon from his grandfather's blueprints. It looks funky fresh, to be sure, but apparently it's just a regular Splattershot with a fancy paint job.

Weapon Type: Rapid
Level Unlocked: 3
(Requires Inkling Squid amiibo)

Notes:
The Hero Shot Replica is just a different skin for the Splattershot. Do you feel like a hero? Do you want to feel slightly superior to normal Splattershot users? Consider the Hero Shot Replica.

Cost: 1,200
Base Damage: 36

Hero Roller Replica

Weapon Stats:

Range	55
Ink Speed	50
Handling	40

 Sub Weapon:
Suction Bomb

 Special:
Killer Wail

Description:
A sweet replica created by Sheldon from his grandfather's blueprints. It looks funky fresh, to be sure, but apparently it's just a regular Splat Roller with a fancy paint job.

Notes:
Statistically, this roller is exactly the same as the Splat Roller, with the same sub and special weapons. But aesthetically the roller looks much more stylish—your opponents will admire the weapon as you roll over them.

Weapon Type: Roller
Level Unlocked: 3
(Requires Inkling Boy amiibo)
Cost: 1,200
Splash Damage: 25-125
Roll Damage: 140

Hero Charger Replica

Weapon Stats:

Range	85
Charge Speed	50
Mobility	40

 Sub Weapon:
Splat Bomb

 Special:
Bomb Rush

Description:
A sweet replica created by Sheldon from his grandfather's blueprints. It looks funky fresh, to be sure, but apparently it's just a regular Splat Charger with a fancy paint job.

Notes:
The Hero Charger Replica shares stats and sub weapons with the Splat Charger—but it looks cooler!

Weapon Type: Charger
Level Unlocked: 3
(Requires Inkling Girl amiibo)
Cost: 1,200
No Charge Damage: 40
Full Charge Damage: 160

SUB WEAPONS

Every primary weapon is paired with a sub weapon. Whether it comes to spreading ink, detecting enemies, or supplying your team with a forward jump point, sub weapons come in handy in a variety of situations. Each sub weapon consumes ink. So before deploying one, make sure you have enough ink in your ink tank, carried on your character's back. Some sub weapons can be thrown. Hold down the sub weapon button to reveal the weapon's arc-like trajectory. This allows you to deploy each device with greater precision, particularly when lobbing them over great distances or bouncing them off walls and other surfaces.

Tip

The triangle icon on your ink tank's fill gauge represents how much ink it takes to deploy your equipped sub weapon. The ink consumed by each sub weapon varies, as indicated by this icon. But expect each toss to eat up at least half of your ink—swim through your own ink to rapidly replenish your ink tank.

Splat Bomb

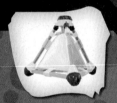

Availability:

- Splattershot Jr.
- Splat Charger
- Splattershot Pro
- Splatterscope
- Dual Squelcher
- Gold Dynamo Roller

These ink-filled pyramid-shaped explosives operate on a time-delayed fuse. Once tossed, they bounce around for a few seconds before exploding, spreading ink over a wide area. This allows them to be bounced around corners, rolled down inclines, or skipped across platforms. While the delayed fuse allows for a variety of deployment techniques, it also gives opponents time to get away. For best results, toss Splat Bombs in areas where opponents are unlikely to see them until it's too late, such as the base of ramps. Splat Bombs only explode on the ground and will not detonate in mid-air.

Tip

The Splat Bomb's fuse begins counting down when it first touches an object—the fuse is paused whenever the Splat Bomb is falling, then resumes the countdown when it lands. When throwing a Splat Bomb downward at an opponent, bounce it off a ledge to begin the timer. Then when it lands, your opponent has less time to get away.

Burst Bomb

Availability:

- Splattershot
- Custom Jet Squelcher
- E-Liter 3K

Think of these sub weapons as water balloons filled with ink. Although they lack the blast radius of Splat Bombs, Burst Bombs explode on contact. But they inflict very little damage, even when scoring a direct hit. This makes Burst Bombs best suited for spreading ink and applying touch-ups. But unlike Splat Bombs, Burst Bombs consume less ink, allowing you to deploy them with greater frequency. You can toss two or three Burst Bombs in quick succession without depleting your ink tank. This comes in handy when you need to make a quick escape. Toss a few Burst Bombs in the direction of your opponent before swimming to safety.

Disruptor

Availability:

- Custom Splattershot Jr.
- Blaster

When an opponent is hit with a Disruptor, their speed is decreased significantly, making them an easy target—they're also surrounded by several swimming squid icons, making them easy to spot, even when swimming. In addition to reducing their speed, Disruptor also increases the ink consumption of their weapons while reducing the rate at which their ink tank is replenished. In short, this is a great way to disable opponents. The Disruptor has a sphere-like blast radius. Any opponents caught within this sphere are affected. For best results, toss these in congested areas like chokepoints or Splat Zones where you're likely to affect multiple opponents.

Suction Bomb

Availability:

- Splat Roller
- Tentatek Splattershot
- Rapid Blaster Deco

As their name implies, Suction Bombs stick to any vertical or horizontal surface they touch before exploding after a short delay, spreading ink over a wide area. These devices have a slightly longer fuse than Splat Bombs—the base of the Suction Bomb flashes repeatedly just before it explodes. The ink coverage of a Suction Bomb is similar to a Splat Bomb, but their ability to stick to surfaces allows you to plant them in spots your enemies might not suspect. Instead of tossing them on the ground, stick them to walls, just above an opponent's eye level—opponents are less likely to expect explosives on walls.

Sprinkler

Availability:

- Kelp Splat Charger
- .96 Gal
- Dynamo Roller
- Kelp Splatterscope

This device functions just like a lawn sprinkler, spreading ink over a modest 360-degree radius. The narrow streams of ink don't inflict much damage, but Sprinklers are a good way to maintain ink coverage in high-traffic areas during both Turf War and Splat Zones. Instead of tossing it on the ground, where it's likely to be spotted and destroyed, consider throwing it high on a wall—it will stick to any surface, like a Suction Bomb. But you can only deploy one Sprinkler at a time. If you toss a second one out, the first one will disappear. Enemy Sprinklers can be destroyed by shooting them. If left untouched, a Sprinkler will continue spreading ink indefinitely.

Point Sensor

Availability:

- Classic Squiffer
- Custom Blaster
- Forge Splattershot Pro

The Point Sensor is like a miniaturized version of the Echolocator special. This hand-tossed device emits a sphere-shaped radius, effectively tagging any opponent within for twelve seconds. During this period, the tagged opponent can be seen by you and your teammates at all times. Your target is constantly circled by a squid icon. This squid animation appears on your team's screens, even if the opponent is swimming or hidden behind a wall. This makes it much easier to track down and eliminate opponents.

Squid Beakon

Availability:

- Krak-On Splat Roller

This radar-like device can be dropped to give your team a jump point on the stage. Squid Beakons appear on the GamePad's map as radar icons. Simply select one of these icons to initiate a Super Jump toward the selected Beakon. Once a player lands on a Squid Beakon, it explodes—so don't be stingy with these things. Keep deploying more Squid Beakons to give your team an advantage. For best results, place Squid Beakons in safe areas near the center of a stage. This gives your team quick access to hotly contested areas like Splat Zones. The GamePad's map also shows enemy Squid Beakons. Use this intel to hunt down the enemy's Squid Beakons—they can be destroyed by shooting them. Or simply camp an enemy Squid Beakon and ambush an opponent as they jump into view. Each player can place up to three Squid Beakons on a stage at a time. If all eight players have Squid Beakons, that means there can be up to twenty-four Squid Beakons on a stage at any given time.

Seeker

Availability:

- Aerospray MG
- .52 Gal Deco

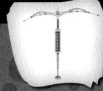

Seekers run along the ground, spreading a narrow linear line of ink behind them—swim through this ink trail to quickly get around a stage. In their default mode, Seekers continue moving in a straight line until they hit an object, at which point they explode. But Seekers can also lock on to opponents. Hold down the sub weapon button to lock on to visible opponents—a reticle appears over your target. Release the sub weapon button to send the Seeker toward your target. While Seekers will attempt to chase down your target, they're incapable of making sharp turns or traversing steep inclines. But they can zoom right up most ramps, perfect for surprising opponents on the other side.

Note

It's possible, but difficult, to jump over an enemy Seeker. It's best to simply hide behind a wall. The Bubbler and Kraken specials can nullify Seekers, preventing them from exploding and spreading ink.

Splash Wall

Availability:

- .52 Gal
- Jet Squelcher

This defensive wall rains down ink, blocking enemy movement and incoming ink. However, you can still shoot through your team's Splash Walls, making them an absolute game changer during duels, particularly in tight chokepoints. The Splash Wall is powered by its own integrated ink tank, visible along the center vertical pole. The ink level drops the longer the Splash Wall has been deployed—it takes approximately seven seconds for a Splash Wall to fully consume its ink. As enemy ink strikes the wall, the ink within the tank is depleted at a faster rate.

Ink Mine

Availability:

- New Squiffer
- Aerospray RG
- Rapid Blaster

These devices are placed on the ground and remain in place until they explode. Ink Mines are triggered by enemy movement, but they will also explode on their own if enemy movement hasn't been detected within approximately ten seconds. Drop Ink Mines in high-traffic chokepoints where enemy movement is guaranteed—paths leading out of the opposing team's spawn point are effective. They're also effective when dropped at the top of heavily traversed walls. To avoid getting surprised by enemy Ink Mines, stay within friendly ink. When coated with your team's ink, an enemy Ink Mine will become visible and explode, spreading enemy ink over a wide area. So keep your distance from these mines, even when you've uncovered one.

SPECIALS

Unlike sub weapons, specials aren't readily available at the start of a match. Instead, you must earn the special by inking territory. The more territory you ink, the faster the circular special gauge fills, located in the upper-right corner of the screen. Once the special gauge is full, you can activate your special. But when and where you activate a special is important. Specials grant you a variety of offensive and defensive bonuses, but these bonuses only remain active for a few seconds. On the other hand, if you're splatted while a special is ready, you'll lose the special and progress on the special gauge when you respawn. So don't wait too long to use those specials.

Tip

As soon as you activate a special, you fully replenish the ink in your tank.

Bubbler

Availability:

- Splattershot Jr.
- Classic Squiffer
- Rapid Blaster
- Custom Blaster

You can never go wrong with Bubbler. When activated, a small impenetrable bubble appears around your character, rendering you invincible for approximately five seconds. Bubbler can also be shared with teammates. When activating Bubbler next to a teammate, they'll also get a protective bubble around them. You can also run into a teammate while Bubbler is active to give them Bubbler too—but it will only be active for the same remaining time as yours. So make an effort to seek out a teammate before activating this special. Due to its relatively limited duration, only activate Bubbler when you absolutely need it, such as the beginning of a firefight with an opponent. Bubbler is also effective when entering known high-traffic areas such as Splat Zones and chokepoints where you know enemy ink is flying.

Caution

Stay clear of ledges when Bubbler is active. Although you can't take damage, getting hit with powerful, high-impact weapons like Blasters or Splat Bombs can push you back, potentially knocking you off a ledge. It is possible for all weapons to push you back, or at least stall you, while the Bubbler is active.

Bomb Rush

Availability:

- Splattershot
- Splat Charger
- Splatterscope
- Rapid Blaster Deco

Activating Bomb Rush allows you to deploy unlimited sub weapons, including Splat Bombs, Burst Bombs, and Suction Bombs. This special remains active for approximately six seconds. During this time, continually spam sub weapons in an effort to take out opponents and spread ink—don't worry, you won't run out of ink while Bomb Rush is active. During Turf War, a last-minute push with Bomb Rush can make all the difference, especially if using Splat Bombs or Suction Bombs, covering ink over a wide area before the opposing team can respond.

Echolocator

Availability:

- Custom Splattershot Jr.
- .96 Gal
- Dynamo Roller
- Dual Squelcher
- E-Liter 3K

Echolocator instantly reveals the locations of all opponents on the stage for approximately twelve seconds. And it doesn't just work for you. Your teammates can see the locations of the enemy too. Opponents are shown on the screen as circling squid icons. The lines extending from your character's feet show the direction in which each opponent is located—so even if an enemy is behind you, you get an indicator. With a quick glimpse, you can see exactly where each enemy is positioned. Use Echolocator in conjunction with a teammate's Killer Wail or Inkstrike. By knowing the locations of each enemy, aiming the Killer Wail and Inkstrike specials is much easier, resulting in more splatted opponents.

Killer Wail

Availability:

- Splat Roller
- Kelp Splat Charger
- .52 Gal
- Blaster
- Kelp Splatterscope

Killer Wail is an extremely powerful special, ideal for splatting opponents caught within its lethal sonic cone. When activated, you're prompted to aim the device, which appears like a large megaphone. In addition to rotating the device, you can also tilt it, aiming it up or down. Once set, shoot the Killer Wail to send a sonic blast through the stage. This wave travels through the entire stage, passing through walls and other objects. Given the special's linear attack, aim it down narrow corridors or high-traffic chokepoints. While the Killer Wail doesn't spread ink, any opponents unlucky enough to be caught within its blast will explode, spreading your team's ink over a small area.

Inkzooka

Availability:

- Tentatek Splattershot
- Aerospray MG
- New Squiffer
- Forge Splattershot Pro

This shoulder-fired bazooka-like weapon fires swirling tornados of ink, instantly splatting opponents and leaving behind a narrow ink trail. This is by no means a precision weapon, but while active, you can fire the Inkzooka continuously for approximately six seconds, sending multiple twisters of ink across the stage. But be careful where you fire the Inkzooka. The recoil of each shot nudges you backward. If you're standing near a ledge, this recoil may knock you off the side of the stage. You could also get pushed backward into enemy ink, so make sure the area around your feet is thoroughly coated in your team's ink. The Inkzooka is also difficult to fire when aiming down over a ledge. For best results, activate Inkzooka when you're on the same level as your opponent or just below them.

Kraken

Availability:

- Krak-On Splat Roller
- Custom Jet Squelcher

Activating Kraken transforms your character into a large, invincible squid for approximately six seconds. While in Kraken form, you can swim around a stage (including all inked and non-inked surfaces) leaving behind an ink trail your team can utilize to push deeper into enemy territory. You can also jump, taking out opponents in your path. You must jump to perform a lethal melee strike—simply bumping opponents will only push them around, inflicting no damage. But just like swimming in squid form, you can't cross over mesh walkways or grates while Kraken is active. If you attempt to swim over a grate, you will just fall through. This is an excellent way to avoid a pursuing enemy Kraken—rush over a grate to escape.

Inkstrike

Availability:

- Jet Squelcher
- Splattershot Pro
- .52 Gal Deco
- Aerospray RG
- Gold Dynamo Roller

When Inkstrike is activated, you're prompted to choose a target area on the GamePad's map. While choosing a target, your character remains still and is extremely vulnerable to attack, so find a safe corner before initiating Inkstrike. Once a target area is selected, a large, ink-filled missile fires off your character's back. Upon impact, the missile unleashes a tornado of ink, swirling about and spreading ink over a wide area. This makes Inkstrike extremely effective during Splat Zones. One Inkstrike can usually contest or outright capture an enemy-held Splat Zone. If you're on the receiving end of an Inkstrike, watch for the swirling indicator on the ground—this is your cue to escape before the missile impacts. When possible, swim away from an incoming Inkstrike—you're taking a risk if you try to outrun the ink tornado.

ABILITIES

| All clothing, shoes, and headgear have a fixed main ability and up to three sub abilities. Once you've earned enough BP, a sub ability slot is unlocked and a random ability is applied. This occurs immediately following matches.

Before diving in to clothing, shoes, and headgear, it's important to understand the fundamentals of the abilities associated with these items. Each piece of gear worn by your character has one main ability associated with it. Items also have three sub ability slots—sub abilities are earned by accruing BP, after which a random sub ability is assigned to the item. However, main abilities are three times as potent as sub abilities. So when choosing gear, focus on its main ability—the sub abilities are just a nice bonus. Both main and sub abilities work together, applying a variety of benefits to your character. Here's a complete listing of all abilities as well as an explanation of how they function in the game.

Tip

When customizing your character's loadout, first find a weapon that fits your style of play. Next, choose abilities (through the purchase of clothes, shoes, and headgear) that complement your weapon and play style.

Damage Up

Description: Increases damage of your main, sub, and special weapons.

Damage Up increases the damage of main, sub, and special weapons up to 130%. However, weapons cannot pass their innate "number of hits to splat" threshold. For example, Aerospray MG has a base damage of 24.5, meaning that it takes five shots to splat at base. It cannot drop below this number, so Damage Up will cap its damage at 24.9, so it still takes five shots to splat. Damage Up is most useful when using weapons with a high rate of fire or those on the lower threshold of their "number of hits to splat." This is ideal for countering opponents equipped with Defense Up.

148

Defense Up

Description: Reduces damage taken from all attacks.

This ability reduces damage taken from all direct attacks up to 120%. Unlike Damage Up, it can lower thresholds on enemy weapons. For example, the .52 Gal does 52 base damage, which is a two-shot splat. Defense Up can drop the weapon below 50 damage, making it a three-shot splat with the .52 Gal. This is one of the most valuable abilities, particularly if you're new to the game, decreasing the effectiveness of your opponents' weapons. Players with an aggressive play style also benefit from Defense Up.

Ink Saver (Main)

Description: Decreases the amount of ink consumed by your main weapon.

Ink Saver (Main) decreases ink usage of your main weapon by up to 60% of its normal usage. For example, a weapon that normally can continuously fire for 17 seconds becomes able to fire for just more than 27 seconds. This is useful when using roller-based weapons, increasing the distance you can roll before refilling your ink tank. Generally, the ability is great in Turf War, allowing you to spread more ink with fewer interruptions.

Ink Saver (Sub)

Description: Decreases the amount of ink consumed by your sub weapon.

This ability decreases ink usage of your sub weapon by up to 75% of its normal usage. The sub weapon's revised ink usage is indicated by a red arrow icon on your character's ink tank. This allows you to deploy sub weapons, like Splat Bombs and Burst Bombs, with greater frequency.

Ink Recovery Up

Description: Increases ink tank refill rate while in squid form.

Ink Recovery Up increases your ink tank's refill rate by up to 40%, but only while in squid form—and you don't need to be swimming to gain this benefit. So if you find yourself running out of ink quickly, consider equipping this ability.

Run Speed Up

Description: Increases movement speed while in Inkling form.

Run Speed Up increases your movement speed by up to 50% when in Inkling form. This affects movement while running and while firing your weapon. However, it does not affect rolling speed with roller-type weapons. Still, this is one of the more effective abilities, particularly when rushing objectives like Splat Zones during the opening moments of a match.

Swim Speed Up

Description: Increases movement speed while in squid form.

This ability increases squid form movement by up to 25%. This also affects movement speed while under the effect of the Kraken special. Like Run Speed Up, this ability comes in handy during those opening moments in a match when you're pushing toward a stage's center. This can help you reach objectives or contested areas before your opponents. The ability can also be a life saver when escaping attacks.

Special Charge Up

Description: Increases special-gauge fill rate.

Special Charge Up increases the rate at which the special gauge fills by up to 30%, allowing for more frequent deployment of specials. But you still need to spread ink to fill that gauge. This makes the ability most effective in Turf War, where you're already tasked with spreading ink.

Special Duration Up

Description: Increases usage time of special weapons.

This ability increases the duration of special weapons—the effects of Bubbler, Inkzooka, Kraken, Bomb Rush, and Echolocator all last longer. For Inkstrike and Killer Wail you're only given more time to aim the weapon, but the effect itself does not last longer. When Bubbler is extended to teammates, they also benefit from the increased duration, even if they don't have the Special Duration Up ability.

Quick Respawn

Description: Decreases respawn time after getting splatted.

After getting splatted, Quick Respawn decreases the time spent watching the splat cam by up to 66%. Normally watching the splat cam takes six seconds, followed by a three-second respawn animation, for a combined nine-second respawn time. This ability only reduces the splat cam portion of the respawn process. With Quick Respawn, the splat cam portion is reduced to four seconds, for a seven-second respawn time. If fully stacked with three Quick Respawn abilities equipped, the splat cam portion is reduced to two seconds, for a five-second respawn time.

Special Saver

Description: Reduces the amount your special gauge decreases after getting splatted.

Each time you get splatted, your special gauge is reduced. This ability reduces the special gauge loss after death by up to 100%. Normally you lose 50% of your special gauge upon death, but if you fully stack Special Saver, you lose nothing. This ability is very helpful for those times when you get splatted just before being rewarded a special.

Quick Super Jump

Description: Your Super Jumps are faster.

Quick Super Jump increases your Super Jump speed by up to double the normal rate, allowing for quicker deployment when jumping to teammates or Squid Beakons.

Bomb Range Up

Description: Bombs, Point Sensors, and Disruptors travel farther when thrown.

This ability allows you to throw Splat Bombs, Burst Bombs, Suction Bombs, Point Sensors, and Disruptors up to 50% farther. The visible arc shown when tossing these weapons is noticeably extended, allowing you to toss these weapons impressive distances. Sometimes you can toss these weapons at greater distances than your opponents can shoot you. This allows you to stand just outside their weapon's range while retaliating with bombs.

Opening Gambit

Description: Boosts your speed in both Inkling and squid form for the first 30 seconds of battle.

Opening Gambit increases the Run Speed Up and Swim Speed Up parameters for the first 30 seconds of the match, allowing you to move much faster. This is ideal for reaching objectives and contested chokepoints before your opponents during the opening moments of a match. This ability is restricted to headgear as a main ability.

Last-Ditch Effort

Description: Boosts ink recovery rate and weapon ink efficiency for the last 30 seconds of the match.

This ability gives you a significant boost during the final seconds of each match, increasing Ink Saver (Main), Ink Saver (Sub), and Ink Recovery Up parameters. This makes you less likely to run out of ink, ideal for making aggressive last-second pushes during Turf War. This ability is restricted to headgear as a main ability.

Tenacity

Description: Fills special gauge automatically if your team has fewer active players than the enemy.

Tenacity fills your special gauge automatically if your team has more inactive players than the enemy team. A player is flagged as inactive while waiting to respawn—inactive players are shown at the top of the screen, represented by squids with X shapes over their eyes. The more inactive players your team has, in comparison to the opposing team, the faster your special gauge fills. This ability is restricted to headgear as a main ability.

Comeback

Description: After respawning, some of your abilities are boosted for a short time.

Comeback increases Ink Saver (Main), Ink Saver (Sub), Ink Recovery Up, Run Speed Up, and Swim Speed Up parameters for 20 seconds after respawning. The decreased ink consumption and increased speed bonuses make you a formidable threat when charging out of your spawn point or Super Jumping to a contested area on the stage. This ability is restricted to headgear as a main ability.

Cold Blooded

Description: Shortens the effect of attacks that let enemies track your position, such as Point Sensors.

This ability is restricted to clothing and shortens the effect of position-tracking attacks substantially. Point Sensor is reduced from 10 to 2.5 seconds. Echolocator and Haunt are reduced from 12 to 3 seconds. So if you prefer to remain hidden, Cold Blooded may be the ability for you. This ability is restricted to clothing as a main ability.

Ninja Squid

Description: Leaves no trace when swimming in inked ground, but reduces swim speed slightly.

With Ninja Squid equipped, you leave no trace while swimming on horizontal surfaces and ramps in squid form. However, you're still visible while swimming on vertical walls. The reduction in swim speed for each is negligible. This ability is perfect for sneaking up on opponents or making stealthy escapes. This ability is restricted to clothing as a main ability.

Haunt

Description: If you get splatted, the position of the player who got you will be visible to your team.

Haunt marks the opponent that defeated you with a position-tracking mark for 12 seconds. This mark can be seen by you and your entire team, similar to Point Sensor or Echolocator. So if you're the type of player who holds a grudge, Haunt is a great way to get your revenge. This ability is restricted to clothing as a main ability.

Recon

Description: You can see the opposing team on the map while standing on the start point.

Recon allows you (but not your team members) to see the opposing team on the GamePad's map while you're standing on your team's spawn point. Use this intel to plan out your attack before moving out. Or, if playing in the same room as your teammates, stand on your team's spawn point and call out enemy positions. This ability is restricted to clothing as a main ability.

Bomb Sniffer

Description: Traps and hidden bombs set by your opponents are visible.

This ability is restricted to shoes and allows you to see Ink Mines that are hidden by opponents. All bombs (including Ink Mines) within a certain distance appear as skull icons on your screen. These skull icons can be seen through walls, so you can tell if opponents are throwing bombs around a corner at you. This ability is restricted to shoes as a main ability.

Ink Resistance Up

Description: Damage and movement penalties incurred when moving through enemy ink are reduced.

Normally, you take 50 damage over three seconds while standing in enemy ink. Your movement speed is reduced to 12.5% of normal and you suffer a 60% reduction in jump speed and height as well. Ink Resistance Up changes all of this. When equipped, you only take a maximum of 25 damage when standing in enemy ink for six seconds. Your movement speed is reduced to 80% of normal and your jump speed and height are unaffected. This is clearly one of the most effective abilities thanks in large part to the reduction in the mobility penalties applied when moving through enemy ink. This ability is restricted to shoes as a main ability.

Stealth Jump

Description: Your Super Jump landing points are hidden, but your Super Jumps are slower.

Normally when performing a Super Jump, a marker appears on the ground where you're about to land, which is visible to all players, including opponents. Stealth Jump hides this landing point marker. Your Super Jump speed is slightly reduced, but the decrease is negligible. This ability is restricted to shoes as a main ability.

Tip

If you're not satisfied with an item's randomized sub abilities, speak with Spyke in the Plaza. For the price of one Super Sea Snail, Spyke will let you reroll the sub abilities on a piece of gear. But remember, all sub abilities slots will be rerolled—you can't just reroll one slot at a time.

Press X while a piece of equipment is selected to reveal details on its rarity, main ability, and sub abilities.

Think of the clothing, shoes, and headgear worn by your Inkling as armor. Each equipped piece of gear grants your character one main ability and as many as three sub abilities. If completely outfitted with rare (three star) clothing, shoes, and headgear, this means your character can go into ink battles benefitting from three main abilities and nine sub abilities. This array of abilities all works together, improving your performance in various ways. But don't get obsessed with collecting rare gear. Gear with one or two-star rarity can be upgraded by paying Spyke Super Sea Snails, adding additional sub ability slots.

Note

Unlike Ammo Knights, the gear shops change their stock each day. Their available stock is based on your level. However, the only thing level affects is the rarity of the equipment that shows up each day—level 20 is required for the rarest equipment to have a chance of showing up.

Understanding Gear

Varsity Jacket

Brand — Zekko

Main Ability

Damage Up

Sub Abilities

Rarity

BP

Main Ability

Each piece of gear has one main ability. The main ability is three times as potent as a sub ability. Main abilities are static and cannot be changed.

Rarity

The rarity of the gear ranges from one to three stars, with one star being the most common and three stars being the rarest. The rarity of gear directly correlates to the number of unlocked sub ability slots it starts with—one-star gear gets only one sub ability slot, two-star gear gets two slots, and three-star gear gets three slots. The rarity also determines the amount of BP needed to unlock each sub ability.

Brand

An item's brand can influence which sub abilities are assigned. Read up on the Brands for more information.

Sub Abilities

An item's rarity determines the number of its starting sub ability slots. But more sub ability slots can be purchased from Spyke. These abilities are far less powerful than the main ability, but every little bit helps, right? Plus, you can have up to nine of these sub abilities.

BP

This meter shows how much BP is required to unlock the next sub ability. BP is awarded at the end of each match. If enough BP is earned to unlock a sub ability, the ability is randomized and added to the gear.

Brands

> *In addition to an item's rarity, pay close attention to its brand, especially if you want certain sub abilities.*

All clothing, shoes, and headgear are manufactured by different brands. Each brand has two weighted abilities: a common ability and an uncommon ability. The common ability is five times more likely to appear as a sub ability for that brand when compared to other brands. For example, Damage Up is five times more likely to appear on SquidForce-branded gear compared to every other brand, except Inkline. The uncommon ability is half as likely to appear as a sub ability for that brand when compared to other brands. For example, Damage Up is half as likely to appear on Inkline-branded gear compared to every other brand, except SquidForce. Branded equipment from KOG, Cuttlegear, and amiibo don't have common or uncommon abilities—every ability has an equal chance of appearing. So if attempting to roll specific sub abilities for your gear, pay close attention to the brand. This will help determine the likelihood of rolling the sub abilities you want.

Brand Weights

Brand	Name	Common Ability (5X)	Uncommon Ability (½X)
	amiibo	—	—
	Cuttlegear	—	—
	Firefin	Ink Saver (Sub)	Ink Recovery Up
	Forge	Special Duration Up	Ink Saver (Sub)
	Inkline	Defense Up	Damage Up
	KOG	—	—
	Krak-On	Swim Speed Up	Defense Up
	Rockenberg	Run Speed Up	Swim Speed Up
	Skalop	Quick Respawn	Special Saver

156

Brand Weights (continued)

Brand	Name	Common Ability (5X)	Uncommon Ability (½X)
GiMN	Splash Mob	Ink Saver (Main)	Run Speed Up
SquidForce	SquidForce	Damage Up	Ink Saver (Main)
Takoroka	Takoroka	Special Charge Up	Special Duration Up
Tentatek	Tentatek	Ink Recovery Up	Quick Super Jump
Zekko	Zekko	Special Saver	Special Charge Up
Zink	Zink	Quick Super Jump	Quick Respawn

Clothing

Visit Jelonzo at Jelly Fresh to see what clothing he has in stock.
Check back every day to see what new items are available.

Jelly Fresh Inventory

Gear	Name	Main Ability	Brand	Rarity	Cost	Special Criteria
	Aloha Shirt	Ink Recovery Up	Forge	☆	700	—
	Anchor Sweat	Cold-Blooded	SquidForce	☆☆	3,000	—
	Baby-Jelly Shirt	Defense Up	Splash Mob	☆☆	2,200	—
	Baseball Jersey	Special Charge Up	Firefin	☆☆☆	10,000	—
	Basic Tee	Quick Respawn	SquidForce	☆	0	—
	B-ball Jersey (Away)	Ink Saver (Sub)	Zink	☆	800	—
	B-ball Jersey (Home)	Special Saver	Zink	☆☆	2,300	—
	Berry Ski Jacket	Special Duration Up	Inkline	☆☆	3,000	—
	Black 8-Bit FishFry	Defense Up	Firefin	☆	600	—
	Black Anchor Tee	Recon	SquidForce	☆☆	2,800	—
	Black Baseball LS	Swim Speed Up	Rockenberg	☆	800	—
	Black Layered LS	Ink Saver (Main)	SquidForce	☆	500	—

157

Gear	Name	Main Ability	Brand	Rarity	Cost	Special Criteria
	Black LS	Quick Super Jump	Zekko	⭐⭐	3,000	—
	Black Pipe Tee	Special Saver	KOG	⭐	800	—
	Black Squideye	Run Speed Up	Tentatek	⭐	500	—
	Black Tee	Special Duration Up	SquidForce	⭐	400	—
	Blue Peaks Tee	Ink Saver (Sub)	Inkline	⭐	400	—
	Camo Layered LS	Special Charge Up	SquidForce	⭐	600	—
	Camo Zip Hoodie	Quick Respawn	Firefin	⭐⭐⭐	9,000	—
	Choco Layered LS	Ink Saver (Sub)	Takoroka	⭐⭐	1,800	—
	Dark Urban Vest	Cold-Blooded	Firefin	⭐⭐⭐	10,000	—
	Firefin Navy Sweat	Bomb Range Up	Firefin	⭐⭐	2,500	—
	Grape Tee	Ink Recovery Up	Skalop	⭐	400	—
	Gray College Sweat	Swim Speed Up	Splash Mob	⭐	800	—
	Gray Vector Tee	Quick Super Jump	Takoroka	⭐	500	—
	Green Striped LS	Ninja Squid	Inkline	⭐	700	—
	Green Zip Hoodie	Special Duration Up	Firefin	⭐⭐	2,800	—
	Green-Check Shirt	Bomb Range Up	Zekko	⭐⭐	2,000	—
	Hero Jacket Replica	Swim Speed Up	Cuttlegear	⭐⭐	0	Complete the Single-Player mode
	Ivory Peaks Tee	Haunt	Inkline	⭐	400	—
	Layered Vector LS	Special Saver	Takoroka	⭐⭐	2,500	—
	Linen Shirt	Bomb Range Up	Splash Mob	⭐	700	—
	Mint Tee	Defense Up	Skalop	⭐	400	—

Gear	Name	Main Ability	Brand	Rarity	Cost	Special Criteria
	Mountain Vest	Swim Speed Up	Inkline	⭐⭐⭐	11,000	—
	Navy Striped LS	Damage Up	Splash Mob	⭐⭐	2,300	—
	Octoling Armor	Ink Saver (Sub)	Cuttlegear	⭐⭐	0	Complete the Single-Player mode
	Olive Ski Jacket	Recon	Inkline	⭐⭐⭐	11,000	—
	Part-Time Pirate	Damage Up	Tentatek	⭐	800	—
	Pirate-Stripe Tee	Special Duration Up	Splash Mob	⭐	700	—
	Power Armor	Quick Respawn	amiibo	⭐⭐	0	Inkling Squid amiibo: Defeat Octonozzle
	Rainy-Day Tee	Ink Saver (Main)	Krak-On	⭐	300	—
	Red Vector Tee	Ink Saver (Main)	Takaroka	⭐	500	—
	Red-Check Shirt	Ink Saver (Main)	Zekko	⭐⭐	2,000	—
	Retro Sweat	Defense Up	SquidForce	⭐⭐⭐	800	—
	Rockenberg Black	Damage Up	Rockenberg	⭐	800	—
	Rockenberg White	Ink Recovery Up	Rockenberg	⭐⭐	2,500	—
	Sage Polo	Cold-Blooded	Splash Mob	⭐	400	—
	Sailor-Stripe Tee	Run Speed Up	Splash Mob	⭐	700	—
	Samurai Jacket	Special Charge Up	amiibo	⭐⭐	0	Inkling Boy amiibo: Defeat Octonozzle
	School Uniform	Ink Recovery Up	amiibo	⭐⭐	0	Inkling Girl amiibo: Defeat Octonozzle
	Shrimp-Pink Polo	Ninja Squid	Splash Mob	⭐	400	—
	Sky-Blue Squideye	Cold-Blooded	Tentatek	⭐	500	—
	Splatfest Tee	Special Saver	SquidForce	⭐⭐⭐	0	Only obtainable during Splatfests. Removed after Splatfest is over.

Gear	Name	Main Ability	Brand	Rarity	Cost	Special Criteria
	Squidmark LS	Haunt	SquidForce	⭐	600	—
	Squidmark Sweat	Bomb Range Up	SquidForce	⭐	800	—
	Striped Rugby	Run Speed Up	Takaroka	⭐⭐	2,300	—
	Striped Shirt	Quick Super Jump	Splash Mob	⭐⭐	2,200	—
	Sunny-Day Tee	Special Charge Up	Krak-On	⭐	300	—
	Tricolor Rugby	Quick Respawn	Takaroka	⭐	700	—
	Urchins Jersey	Run Speed Up	Zink	⭐	700	—
	Varsity Baseball LS	Recon	Splash Mob	⭐	700	—
	Varsity Jacket	Damage Up	Zekko	⭐⭐⭐	12,000	—
	Vintage Check Shirt	Haunt	Rockenberg	⭐⭐⭐	9,000	—
	White 8-Bit FishFry	Recon	Firefin	⭐	700	—
	White Anchor Tee	Ninja Squid	SquidForce	⭐⭐⭐	8,000	—
	White Baseball LS	Quick Super Jump	Rockenberg	⭐	800	—
	White Layered LS	Special Saver	SquidForce	⭐	500	—
	White Line Tee	Swim Speed Up	KOG	⭐	700	—
	White Shirt	Ink Recovery Up	Splash Mob	⭐⭐	1,800	—
	White Striped LS	Quick Respawn	Splash Mob	⭐⭐	2,300	—
	White Tee	Ink Saver (Sub)	SquidForce	⭐	400	—
	Yellow Layered LS	Quick Super Jump	SquidForce	⭐	500	—
	Yellow Urban Vest	Haunt	Firefin	⭐⭐	3,000	—
	Zekko Baseball LS	Defense Up	Zekko	⭐	800	—
	Zekko Hoodie	Ninja Squid	Zekko	⭐⭐	2,800	—

Jelly Fresh Inventory (continued)

Gear	Name	Main Ability	Brand	Rarity	Cost	Special Criteria
	Zink Layered LS	Damage Up	Zink	⭐	600	—
	Zink LS	Special Duration Up	Zink	⭐	500	—

Shoes

Crusty Sean, over at Fresh Kicks, has plenty of footwear to choose from. Stock is rotated daily, so don't forget to stop by the shop—you just might find that perfect pair you've been waiting for.

Fresh Kicks Inventory

Gear	Name	Main Ability	Brand	Rarity	Cost	Special Criteria
	Banana Basics	Bomb Sniffer	Krak-On	⭐	400	—
	Black Seahorses	Swim Speed Up	Zink	⭐⭐	2,000	—
	Black Trainers	Quick Respawn	Tentatek	⭐	500	—
	Blue Lo-Tops	Defense Up	Zekko	⭐	800	—
	Blue Moto Boots	Ink Resistance Up	Rockenberg	⭐⭐⭐	12,000	—
	Blue Slip-Ons	Bomb Range Up	Krak-On	⭐	300	—
	Blueberry Casuals	Ink Saver (Sub)	Krak-On	⭐	700	—
	Cherry Kicks	Stealth Jump	Rockenberg	⭐⭐	2,800	—
	Choco Clogs	Quick Respawn	Krak-On	⭐⭐	1,800	—
	Clownfish Basics	Special Charge Up	Krak-On	⭐	500	—
	Crazy Arrows	Stealth Jump	Takoroka	⭐⭐⭐	9,000	—
	Cream Basics	Special Saver	Krak-On	⭐	0	—
	Cream Hi-Tops	Stealth Jump	Krak-On	⭐	500	—
	Cyan Trainers	Damage Up	Tentatek	⭐	700	—
	Gold Hi-Horses	Run Speed Up	Zink	⭐⭐	3,000	—

Gear	Name	Main Ability	Brand	Rarity	Cost	Special Criteria
	Hero Runner Replicas	Quick Super Jump	Cuttlegear	★★	0	Complete the Single-Player mode
	Hunter Hi-Tops	Ink Recovery Up	Krak-On	★	500	—
	LE Lo-Tops	Ink Saver (Sub)	Zekko	★★★	8,000	—
	Moto Boots	Quick Respawn	Rockenberg	★★	3,000	—
	Neon Sea Slugs	Ink Resistance Up	Tentatek	★	700	—
	Octoling Boots	Special Saver	Cuttlegear	★★	0	Complete the Single-Player mode
	Orange Arrows	Ink Saver (Main)	Takoroka	★	700	—
	Orange Lo-Tops	Swim Speed Up	Zekko	★	800	—
	Oyster Clogs	Run Speed Up	Krak-On	★	600	—
	Pink Trainers	Bomb Range Up	Tentatek	★	500	—
	Plum Casuals	Damage Up	Krak-On	★★	2,000	—
	Power Boots	Ink Saver (Main)	amiibo	★★	0	Inkling Squid amiibo: Defeat Octowhirl
	Pro Trail Boots	Bomb Sniffer	Inkline	★★★	9.800	—
	Purple Hi-Horses	Special Duration Up	Zink	★	800	—
	Purple Sea Slugs	Run Speed Up	Tentatek	★	800	—
	Red Hi-Horses	Ink Saver (Main)	Zink	★	800	—
	Red Hi-Tops	Ink Resistance Up	Krak-On	★★	1,800	—
	Red Sea Slugs	Special Saver	Tentatek	★★★	3,000	—
	Red Slip-Ons	Quick Super Jump	Krak-On	★	300	—
	Red Work Boots	Quick Super Jump	Rockenberg	★★★	11,000	—
	Samurai Shoes	Special Duration Up	amiibo	★★	0	Inkling Boy amiibo: Defeat Octowhirl

Gear	Name	Main Ability	Brand	Rarity	Cost	Special Criteria
	School Shoes	Ink Saver (Sub)	amiibo	⭐⭐	0	Inkling Girl amiibo: Defeat Octowhirl
	Squid-Stitch Slip-Ons	Defense Up	Krak-On	⭐⭐	1,500	—
	Tan Work Boots	Bomb Range Up	Rockenberg	⭐⭐	3,000	—
	Trail Boots	Ink Recovery Up	Inkline	⭐⭐	2,800	—
	Turquoise Kicks	Special Charge Up	Rockenberg	⭐⭐	2,800	—
	White Arrows	Special Duration Up	Takoroka	⭐⭐	2,500	—
	White Kicks	Swim Speed Up	Rockenberg	⭐	~800	—
	White Seahorses	Ink Recovery Up	Zink	⭐	600	—
	Yellow Seahorses	Bomb Sniffer	Zink	⭐⭐	1,500	—
	Zombie Hi-Horses	Special Charge Up	Zink	⭐	800	—

Headgear

Annie, at Cooler Heads, sells a variety of hats and other headgear. Like the other gear shops, check in with Annie each day to see what new items she has in stock.

Cooler Heads Inventory

Gear	Name	Main Ability	Brand	Rarity	Cost	Special Criteria
	Backwards Cap	Quick Respawn	Zekko	⭐	700	—
	B-ball Headband	Opening Gambit	Zink	⭐	300	—
	Bike Helmet	Ink Recovery Up	Skalop	⭐⭐⭐	11,000	—
	Black Arrowbands	Tenacity	Zekko	⭐⭐	800	—
	Bobble Hat	Quick Super Jump	Splash Mob	⭐⭐	2,000	—
	Camo Mesh	Swim Speed Up	Firefin	⭐⭐	2,500	—
	Camping Hat	Special Duration Up	Inkline	⭐	800	—

Gear	Name	Main Ability	Brand	Rarity	Cost	Special Criteria
	Designer Headphones	Ink Saver (Sub)	Forge	⭐⭐	2,500	—
	Fake Contacts	Special Charge Up	Tentatek	⭐⭐	2,000	—
	FishFry Visor	Special Charge Up	Firefin	⭐	500	—
	Five-Panel Cap	Comeback	Zekko	⭐⭐	2,000	—
	Gas Mask	Tenacity	Forge	⭐⭐⭐	11,000	—
	Golf Visor	Run Speed Up	Zink	⭐	400	—
	Hero Headset Replica	Run Speed Up	Cuttlegear	⭐⭐	0	Complete the Single-Player mode
	Jet Cap	Special Saver	Firefin	⭐	700	—
	Jogging Headband	Ink Saver (Sub)	Zekko	⭐	400	—
	Jungle Hat	Ink Saver (Main)	Firefin	⭐⭐⭐	9,000	—
	Lightweight Cap	Swim Speed Up	Inkline	⭐	700	—
	Octoling Goggles	Bomb Range Up	Cuttlegear	⭐⭐	0	Complete the Single-Player mode
	Paintball Mask	Comeback	Forge	⭐⭐⭐	10,000	—
	Pilot Goggles	Bomb Range Up	Forge	⭐⭐⭐	9,800	—
	Power Mask	Defense Up	amiibo	⭐⭐	0	Inkling Squid amiibo: Defeat Octostomp
	Retro Specs	Quick Respawn	Splash Mob	⭐	500	—
	Safari Hat	Last-Ditch Effort	Forge	⭐⭐	2,300	—
	Samurai Helmet	Damage Up	amiibo	⭐⭐	0	Inkling Boy amiibo: Defeat Octostomp
	Short Beanie	Ink Saver (Main)	Inkline	⭐	600	—
	Skate Helmet	Special Saver	Skalop	⭐⭐	2,500	—
	Snorkel Mask	Damage Up	Forge	⭐⭐	3,000	—

Gear	Name	Main Ability	Brand	Rarity	Cost	Special Criteria
	Splash Goggles	Defense Up	Forge	⭐⭐	2,800	—
	Sporty Bobble Hat	Tenacity	Skalop	⭐	800	—
	Squash Headband	Damage Up	Zink	⭐	400	—
	Squid Hairclip	Swim Speed Up	amiibo	⭐⭐	0	Inkling Girl amiibo: Defeat Octostomp
	Squid-Stitch Cap	Opening Gambit	Skalop	⭐⭐⭐	8,500	—
	Squidvader Cap	Special Charge Up	Skalop	⭐⭐	2,300	—
	Streetstyle Cap	Ink Saver (Sub)	Skalop	⭐	600	—
	Striped Beanie	Opening Gambit	Splash Mob	⭐⭐	1,500	—
	Studio Headphones	Ink Saver (Main)	Forge	⭐⭐	2,800	—
	Takoroka Mesh	Defense Up	Takoroka	⭐	400	—
	Tennis Headband	Comeback	Tentatek	⭐	300	—
	Tentacles Helmet	Run Speed Up	Forge	⭐⭐⭐	11,000	—
	Tinted Shades	Last-Ditch Effort	Zekko	⭐	350	—
	Two-Stripe Mesh	Special Saver	Krak-On	⭐	700	—
	Urchins Cap	Bomb Range Up	Skalop	⭐	600	—
	Visor Skate Helmet	Last-Ditch Effort	Skalop	⭐⭐⭐	10,000	—
	White Arrowbands	Special Duration Up	Zekko	⭐⭐⭐	8,000	—
	White Headband	Ink Recovery Up	SquidForce	⭐	0	—
	Zekko Mesh	Quick Super Jump	Zekko	⭐	500	—

TESTER LOADOUTS

...eed some help choosing your weapons and
...ear? The game's testers have been kind enough
...let you in on a few of their secrets. Here's some
...mple loadouts for different types of weapons.
...e these weapon/ability combinations to get
...e upper hand in any ink battle.

Short-Mid Range: Rapid Fire

Recommended Weapons:

- Splatter Shot Jr.
- Tentatek Splattershot
- Aerospray MG
- Aerospray RG

Recommended Gear:

Gear	Main Ability
Clothing	Ninja Squid
Shoes	Ink Resistance Up
Headgear	Defense Up

You can never go wrong with this combination. One Defense Up turns the two-shots-to-splat .52 Gal into a three-shots-to-splat weapon. The fire rate of the Splattershot Jr. will beat the now three-shots-to splat .52 Gal to lethal damage if you're not standing in the enemy's ink. Similarly, rapid-firing weapons are medium- to short-range, which means you will need to get up close and personal with ranged weapon users. Ninja Squid allows you to close the gap between you and enemies with long-range weapons undetected—just be sure not to climb up walls, as Ninja Squid doesn't activate on vertical surfaces! Finally, there's Ink Resistance Up. Normally, standing in an enemy's ink will inflict 50% damage over three seconds. Ink Resistance Up doubles that length of time and halves the damage cap, dealing only 25% damage over six seconds.

Long Range: Rapid Fire

Recommended Weapons:

- .52 Gal
- Splattershot Pro
- Jet Squelcher
- Dual Squelcher

Recommended Gear:

Gear	Main Ability
Clothing	Run Speed Up
Shoes	Ink Resistance Up
Headgear	Ink Saver (Main)

This combination compensates for the tendency of long-distance rapid-fire weapons to have slower firing rates, slower mobility while firing, and higher ink consumption. Ink Saver Main lets you fire more, reducing ink consumption of these ink-hungry weapons. Run Speed Up gives you more mobility while firing, ideal for making offensive pushes or hasty retreats. Ink Resistance Up is a self-explanatory must-have, reducing damage and the movement penalty while standing in enemy ink.

Recommended Weapons:

- Splat Roller
- Krak-On Splat Roller
- Dynamo Roller
- Gold Dynamo Roller

Recommended Gear:

Gear	Main Ability
Clothing	Ninja Squid
Shoes	Stealth Jump
Headgear	Ink Saver (Main)

Rollers excel at sneak attacks in melee range, so Ninja Squid is a very strong ability for every roller. Being able to sneak around your opponents and then smack them with your roller is very effective. Unlike most other weapons, Ink Resistance Up is not necessary on a roller-type weapon. While traversing ground, you're usually covering that ground by rolling, so you don't have to worry about standing in your opponent's ink too much. Stealth Jump allows you to jump into a skirmish undetected, which can easily give you the advantage. Ink Saver (Main) is recommended due to the roller's innate difference from other weapons when it comes to ink coverage. Most other weapon types involve laying a trail of ink, following that trail as a squid (which refills your ink), and repeating. Roller-type weapons don't get the benefit of becoming a squid while covering ground, so you don't refill your ink as naturally. Ink Saver (Main) can help you roll for longer periods without running out.

Long Range: High-Damage

Recommended Weapons:

- Splat Charger
- Splatterscope
- Kelp Splat Charger
- Kelp Splatterscope

Recommended Gear:

Gear	Main Ability
Clothing	Ninja Squid
Shoes	Ink Resistance Up
Headgear	Ink Saver (Main)

These abilities will help any player infiltrate and escape enemy territory, all the while remaining a steady threat from a distance. Ninja Squid allows you to swim around the stage without leaving a trail in your ink, ideal for sneaking up on enemies or making stealthy escapes. Ink Resistance Up allows you to maintain relatively high mobility, even when trudging through your opponent's ink—the reduction in damage during these instances is also a welcome benefit. Ink Saver (Main) comes in handy for reigning in ink consumption on those ink-hungry long-range weapons. Other valid choices for headgear might be Defense Up, Swim Speed Up, and Run Speed Up, depending on your play style.

Close-Quarter: Blaster

Recommended Weapons:

- Blaster
- Rapid Blaster
- Custom Blaster
- Rapid Blaster Deco

Recommended Gear:

Gear	Main Ability
Clothing	Ninja Squid
Shoes	Bomb Sniffer
Headgear	Damage Up

Damage Up increases splash damage, which is highly variable depending on your equipped blaster weapon. Ninja Squid allows you to stealthily move to close range, where your weapon is most effective. Bomb Sniffer is ideal for detecting bombs and Ink Mines. This is essential when operating in close quarters because your movement speed is extremely slow while firing a blaster weapon. Ink Resistance Up can be substituted on shoes and Defense Up can be substituted on headgear for a more offensive, close-range loadout, perfect for raiding Splat Zones and chokepoints.

AROWANA MALL

OVERVIEW

Arowana Mall is a large linear stage, with most action concentrated in the center. Regardless of game mode, controlling the map's center is the key to victory. There are three main paths leading to the stage's center. You can either rush straight ahead or utilize one of the two flanking corridors. Each team has access to one of these corridors—simply run up the ramp adjacent to your team's base. By controlling the middle of the map and the opposing team's flanking ramp, you can restrict your opponent's movement, pushing your foes back to their base.

Key Locations

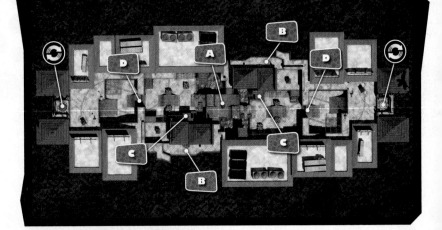

Arowana Mall

Legend

	Spawn Point
	Key Locations

Expect heavy fighting here, in the map's center. While controlling the center is important, avoid loitering on the ground here as you're likely to be hit by incoming ink fired from the perimeter platforms. Either control this area from elevated positions or ink the area and move out fast before you fall victim to enemy ink. If available, use Bubbler when operating in this high-traffic area.

Instead of rushing through the middle of the stage, consider using these two perimeter corridors to reach the map's center. Run up the ramp near your team's base to access this corridor and follow it toward the center. Unless the corridor has been captured by the opposing team (watch for enemy ink) this path is much safer than running up the middle. Plus, each corridor leads to a perch overlooking the center. If you're feeling confident, invade the opposing team's corridor and ambush them as they rush to the center from their base.

These two opposing overwatch platforms are perfect for covering the map's center. Each elevated platform can be accessed via the perimeter corridors adjacent to each team's base. Opponents can only access this platform from behind, meaning they must first access the corridor near your team's base. Consider placing Ink Mines behind you to prevent such sneak attacks.

The ramp leading out of each team's spawn point is a critical chokepoint. Watch out for sneaky opponents setting up ambushes here. Keep an eye on the mini-map and approach this area cautiously if you see enemy ink. The high walls flanking the ramp also serve as excellent sniper perches.

Caution

Be careful when crossing the map's various grates. These grates can't be coated with ink, meaning you can't swim across them in squid form. Furthermore, if you transform into squid form while on a grate, you'll fall through, potentially dropping into the water. Water is a serious threat on this map, so watch your step.

Recommended Weapons

Splat Charger

Given the number of elevated positions, long-range, hard-hitting weapons like the Splat Charger come in handy for dispatching opponents and spreading ink.

Krak-On Splat Roller

Roller-based weapons, like the Krak-On Splat Roller, work well on this map, as the ramps aren't much of an impediment.

Seeker

Due to the numerous ramps on this stage, the Seeker sub weapon is ideal for spreading ink and scoring sneak attacks.

Killer Wail

Killer Wail is a great special when defending narrow chokepoints, like the perimeter corridors. If the enemy has taken control of your team's corridor, use Killer Wail to clear a path.

Tip

When fighting from elevated positions, avoid loadouts with the Inkzooka. It's difficult to aim down with this weapon, making it nearly impossible to hit opponents on the stage's lower pathways. However, Inkzooka is very effective in the perimeter corridors and central chokepoints.

TURF WAR

Arowana Mall

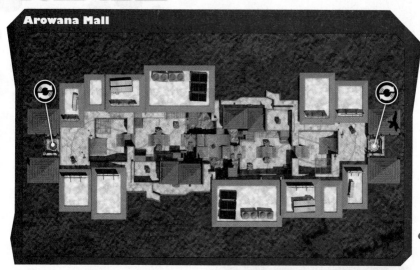

In Turf War, it's all about coverage. So instead of hunting down your opponents, focus on covering as much horizontal territory with ink as you can. While most fighting gravitates around the stage's center, don't overlook the importance of completely coating your team's side of the stage with ink. Also, look for opportunities to sneak into your enemy's territory, using the opponent's corridor. But, as in most game modes, a victory will usually come down to controlling the stage's center. Maintain the high ground and keep the center free of enemies. In close matches, save specials like Inkstrike or Inkzooka to make a last-second push—activate these specials in the final second of a match to help secure a victory.

Legend

⊙	Spawn Point

Remember, every little inch of territory counts. So when using a roller-based weapon, be sure to coat every horizontal surface, paying close attention to inking those corners, particularly in less-contested areas around your team's spawn point.

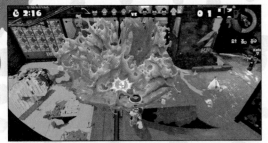

Hide in your ink and look for opportunities to ambush opponents traversing the ramps in the center. Sending Seekers up and over ramps is also an effective way of taking out opponents on the other side.

Even if carrying a roller-based weapon, you can use this ledge at the end of your team's corridor to splat ink across the stage's center. Consider planting Squid Beakons along this corridor to maintain a spawn location near the center of the stage.

Tip

If you suspect opponents are approaching, throw Splat Bombs at the base of ramps. As opponents crest the top of the ramp, they won't see the Splat Bombs until it's too late.

SPLAT ZONES

Arowana Mall

Legend

⊕ Spawn Point	— Splat Zone Boundary

There is one Splat Zone on Arowana Mall, located in the stage's center. Toss Suction Bombs on the kiosk in the center to spread ink and take out opponents. As with any stage with only one Splat Zone, the Inkstrike special is particularly powerful, coating the entire zone with ink and eliminating any opponents unlucky enough to be in the weapon's large blast radius. A well-placed Inkstrike could possibly capture the zone for your team.

Stand on this platform and use a long-range weapon and Splat Bombs to maintain control of the Splat Zone in the center. Ink the platform, then stand on the crate to give your weapon greater range.

These yellow bridges only appear in Splat Zones, providing access to the opposing team's corridor. Use this path to apply pressure on the enemy, keeping them away from the stage's center. But remember, your opponents can apply pressure on your team's corridor too, using the yellow bridge on the opposite side. These bridges make it difficult for snipers to apply pressure on the center as they can be flanked.

Wait until the opposing team has captured the zone, then launch an Inkstrike to help take it back. You may even catch some unfortunate opponents in the large blast.

BLACKBELLY SKATEPARK

OVERVIEW

This sprawling skatepark is filled with ramps and curved surfaces, making roller-based weapons difficult to use here. However, the various elevation changes present some unique tactical opportunities and challenges. For instance, the tall cylindrical platform in the center of the stage offers a sweeping view of the entire skatepark, making it a popular perch for snipers. But don't let the fight over this central platform divert your attention away from the game's objective. Holding the high ground is important, but it won't necessarily guarantee you a victory.

Key Locations

Blackbelly Skatepark

Legend

	Spawn Point
	Key Locations

This central platform is often the focal point of most battles, regardless of game mode. From here sharpshooters can spread ink across the center of the stage as well as engage opponents. The ramp-like inclines on the sides of the platform are the most obvious approach to the top—simply ink the ramps and swim up to reach the top. But it's sneakier to ascend from the front or back side of the platform, accessing the square, rail-enclosed platforms. If the platform is occupied by an opponent, always approach from the front or back side, as these paths are less likely to be watched or booby-trapped with Ink Mines.

These narrow openings on each side of the central platform serve as chokepoints, perfect for ambushing opponents rushing the stage's center. Consider standing on the yellow mesh grate while using the adjoining wall for cover. Using the third-person camera you can see incoming opponents, but they can't see you. Either swim up the wall or peek around it to take your opponents by surprise. From this position you can see the opposing team's spawn point.

Pay close attention to these half pipe areas. The upper ledges of the half pipes can be accessed and inked. Inking these often overlooked areas can make a big difference during close Turf War battles. It's a relatively small area, but in Turf War, every horizontal surface counts. If this area hasn't been inked on the other side of the stage (check your GamePad) sneak over there and claim this ledge for your team. In addition to gaining territory for your team, this can also be a good spot to ambush your opponents. As usual, any height advantage is great for engaging opponents or spreading ink.

Recommended Weapons

Splatterscope

Take the central platform in the center of the stage and use the Splatterscope to pick off opponents at long range. The weapon's scope is ideal for making precise, long-range hits.

Splattershot Jr.

If you're not keen on sniping, you can't go wrong with this jack-of-all-trades. Whether splatting opponents or spreading ink, the Splattershot Jr. (and other Splattershot weapons) is up for the task.

Splat Bomb

When attacking from the central platform, you can lob Splat Bombs great distances, sometimes taking out opponents by surprise. They're also a good way to chase opponents off the central platform.

Inkstrike

Since the central platform is a major point of contention, Inkstrike comes in handy for clearing opponents off the top. Kraken is also very effective for securing the central platform.

TURF WAR

Blackbelly Skatepark

If your team can secure the central platform at the middle of the stage, you stand a good chance of holding out for a victory in Turf War. However, don't neglect the other areas of the stage, including the territory near your team's spawn point. Glance at the GamePad from time to time to ensure the area around your base is covered in your team's ink.

Legend

 Spawn Point

The fight for the central platform can often become a distraction, luring teammates away from the game mode's primary objective, which is coverage. So while everyone rushes to the central platform, look for opportunities to ink the perimeter of the map, including the area near the opposing team's spawn point.

Expect heavy fighting on the central platform. Even if you secure the central platform, you're not safe from attack. Watch out for incoming Splat Bombs and Suction Bombs. Opponents can even swim up the sides of the central platform and take you by surprise. So don't forget to look straight down—opponents gathered at the base of the platform can be difficult to spot.

Roller-based weapons aren't as effective on Blackbelly Skatepark due to the numerous curved surfaces. If using a roller weapon, focus on the flat areas of the stage where the roller can spread the optimal amount of ink. When it comes to covering curved surfaces, swing the roller to splat ink along walls and curves.

Be careful when moving through the perimeter half pipes. Opponents may be hiding behind the walls between the half pipes. Consider tossing a Splat Bomb or other sub weapon ahead before moving through these narrow chokepoints.

Tip

Opponents positioned on the central platform have a difficult time aiming straight down. So if you come under fire, head for the base of the platform to avoid getting hit. However, watch out for incoming Splat Bombs and other sub weapons.

SPLAT ZONES

Blackbelly Skatepark

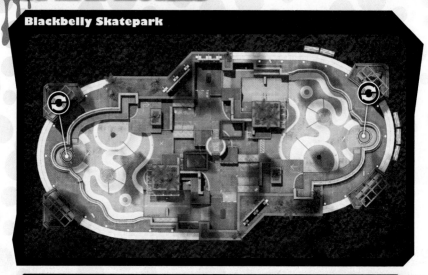

Legend

Spawn Point	— Splat Zone Boundary

There are two Splat Zones on Blackbelly Skatepark, both located near the central platform. While the central platform is not located within either Splat Zone, controlling the central platform is critical—from the top of the central platform you can ink and control both Splat Zones. But don't let the fight over the central platform distract you from the task at hand—capturing the Splat Zones. If you can't maintain control of the platform, attack the Splat Zones from the perimeter platforms. If you're lucky enough to secure both Splat Zones, keep at least two teammates back to defend them while the other team members apply pressure on the opposing team's spawn point.

Don't be surprised if you get picked off by snipers posted on the central platform. Holding the central platform is critical to controlling both Splat Zones. If you can't sneak up on the pesky enemy sniper, use specials like Inkstrike or Kraken to take control of the central platform. Well-placed Splat Bombs and Suction Bombs may also chase a sniper off the top of the central platform.

The central platform isn't the only elevated perch on this stage. Both Splat Zones are surrounded by raised platforms. When you can't secure the central platform, use these perimeter positions to ink the Splat Zones. It's better to attack the Splat Zones from a distance—trudging through the Splat Zones leaves you more open to attacks from above. Consider hiding Squid Beakons near each Splat Zone to maintain a steady presence in the stage's center. Squid Beakons placed on top of the central platform probably won't last long.

Ink a corner just outside a Splat Zone your team controls, then hide in your ink until opponents arrive. When an opponent shows up and begins inking the Splat Zone, pop out of your ink to ambush them. When the threat is eliminated, ink the Splat Zone to recapture it. By guarding just one of the Splat Zones in this fashion, you can help your team secure a victory. It may not be the most sporting way to gain an edge, but it is effective.

SALTSPRAY RIG

OVERVIEW

Saltspray Rig sports a unique layout with both teams spawning on the same side of the stage. Despite its deceptively compact design, the stage is surprisingly large, with several distinct locations consisting of narrow paths, ramps, platforms, and perches. The stage also features multiple elevation changes, making it important to identify and occupy the high ground. There are a few interactive features here too, including two elevator-like platforms in the center, and a platform attached to a crane near the shipping container area. But be careful when traversing these platforms, as they may be watched by opponents.

Key Locations

Saltspray Rig

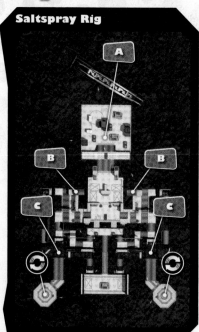

Legend

	Spawn Point
	Key Locations

A Located on the opposite side of the stage from both team's spawn points, this large area is worth capturing and defending, especially during Turf War. There is only one way into this area, making it relatively easy to defend once captured. This area features a few large towers of shipping containers. Ink the sides of these containers and swim to the top to gain a commanding view of this area. There's also a moving mesh platform that allows you to easily transition from one stack of shipping containers to another. This area is most critical during Turf War—it's rarely accessed during Splat Zones. This makes it a good place to plant Squid Beakons, giving your team easy access to the center.

B These two opposing platforms are ideal sniper perches during Splat Zones. From here, snipers can cover the center of the stage and help defend the adjacent shipping container area. But when posted here, keep an eye on the GamePad's map to watch for encroaching ink—this could be the

sign that an enemy is attempting to sneak up behind you. There is more than one way up here, so don't forget to turn around from time to time to apply fresh coats of ink along the surrounding surfaces. Keeping the rear area coated with ink deters enemies from sneaking up on you—Ink Mines are effective too. While you're up here, you may want to ink the nearby diamond-plate ledges as well, particularly during Turf War.

 C These elevated perimeter pathways, just off each team's spawn point, offer a great way to spread ink onto the adjacent lower platforms and ramps. Instead of dropping down to these lower areas, stay on these elevated paths and fire down.

Recommended Weapons

Splattershot Pro

Engagements are unpredictable on this stage, but a good Splattershot will give you a fighting chance. The Pro model offers a good balance of range and damage output.

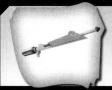

Splat Charger

If you want to occupy one of the two sniper perches, the Splat Charger will serve you well. If you want greater versatility without sacrificing much range, opt for one of the Squelcher weapons.

Splat Bombs

Get to the high ground and lob Splat Bombs down on your opponents. These are useful in all game modes.

Killer Wail

Whether aimed down one of the narrow walkways or up at one of the sniper perches, Killer Wail is great for scattering opponents.

TURF WAR

Saltspray Rig

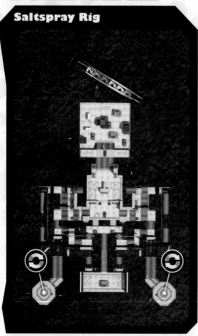

Legend

 Spawn Point

In Turf War, there's a lot of ground to cover on Saltspray Rig. Instead of hunting down opponents, focus on spreading ink. Roller weapons are ideal for coating the narrow paths and ramps near the spawn points—Seekers work well in these areas too. But ranged weapons work best near the stage's center. Here you're likely to encounter snipers on the two perches or on top of the shipping containers in the back area. Avoid getting caught up in sniper duels. Instead, deal with any threats you encounter, then get back to spreading ink. Constantly glance down at the gamepad's map to see areas held by the enemy and respond accordingly.

The area around your team's spawn point is rarely contested, so take a moment to ink this large octagonal platform at the start of the match. Once coated, you probably won't have to apply any touch-ups for the duration of the round. Leaving this area uncovered can lead to a serious disadvantage later when total ink coverage is calculated.

Remember, every horizontal surface counts in Turf War. Sometimes these small platforms and the tops of walls are left uncoated. Ink the vertical pipes or walls to swim to the top of these structures, then apply some ink before moving on. It may not seem like much, but coating small platforms, ledges, and the tops of walls can make a difference during close matches.

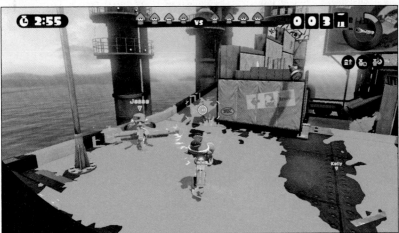

Roller-based weapons are great for quickly coating the narrow corridors and ramps on this stage. If you don't have a roller yourself, follow a teammate who does, applying touch-ups as necessary with a Splattershot weapon. By working together, you can ink large swaths of the stage in a short amount of time. Swim behind your teammate when you're not spreading ink to refill your ink-tank—you'll need to swim to keep up with your speedy teammate.

189

SPLAT ZONES

Saltspray Rig

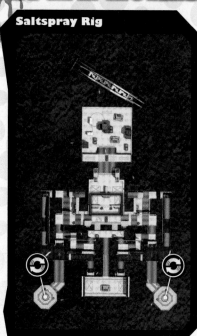

On Saltspray Rig, there is only one large Splat Zone located near the center of the stage, between the two opposing sniper perches. At the start of the round, both teams should rush the center. But instead of moving directly to the Splat Zone, get to at least one of the two sniper perches overlooking the zone. The value of these two positions cannot be overstated. Players equipped with any weapon can spread ink onto the Splat Zone from these elevated positions. If you can't occupy at least one of these perches, you'll have a hard time securing and holding the Splat Zone.

Holding the high ground is essential for maintaining control of the Splat Zone. Take position on one of the sniper perches and fire down on the zone and any opponents who approach. But your presence here won't go unnoticed. Keep the area behind you inked to prevent opponents from sneaking up on you. Snipers posted on the opposing platform also pose a serious threat. If your team can occupy both of these perches, you stand a good chance of winning.

Once your team has secured the zone, look for opportunities to ambush opponents filtering in from their spawn point. Most players take linear, predictable routes toward the center. Consider hiding in your ink at the top or bottom of a ramp and attacking opponents as they rush toward the Splat Zone. Specials like Inkzooka and Killer Wail are particularly useful for slowing down the enemy team's advance.

Both teams spawn a considerable distance from the Splat Zone. Instead of running or swimming toward the center, use Super Jumps to quickly reinforce your teammates. Squid Beakons are also effective for maintaining a presence near the Splat Zone. But before Super Jumping or using a Squid Beakon, monitor the ink situation on the GamePad's map. If your intended jump point is surrounded by enemy ink, reconsider entering the fray—you probably won't last long.

Caution

Avoid using the two elevators near the center of the stage. Riding up the elevators leaves you vulnerable to attacks from above. Don't be surprised if an opponent with a roller is hiding in their ink, waiting for you to come up an elevator. All it takes is one whack with the roller to send you back to your team's spawn point.

URCHIN UNDERPASS

OVERVIEW

In Urchin Underpass, both teams can choose from three narrow paths leading to the stage's high-traffic and chaotic center. While the central path is the most direct, it's also the most predictable. To avoid getting ambushed in the middle, utilize one of the two perimeter paths. Both corridors lead to elevated positions, ideal for spreading ink (and attacking opponents) in the center. Some of the paths here are blocked by vertical nets. You can't walk through these nets, but you can jump through them while in squid form. So make sure both sides of the nets are coated in ink to facilitate fast travel through these areas.

Key Locations

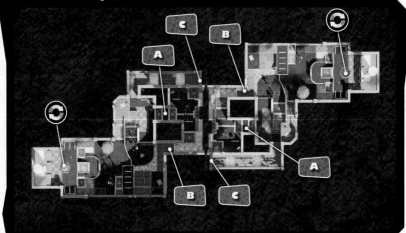

Urchin Underpass

C · A · B

A

B · C

Legend	
⊕	Spawn Point
▬	Key Locations

A As in most stages, the center of Urchin Underpass is hotly contested in every game mode. This area is surrounded by four elevated ledges that both sides can leverage to gain a solid foothold in the center. As a result, when moving through the center, try to swim through your ink to avoid being spotted by opponents camped on these elevated perches. The two central corridors leading here are particularly treacherous. Place a Splash Wall in this corridor in an attempt to prevent your opponents from accessing the center of the stage. Explosive weapons like Splat Bombs and Ink Mines are also effective in these narrow, high-traffic chokepoints.

B Regardless of game mode, reaching the middle of the stage is always important. This narrow, elevated corridor is the quickest way to access the center. From your team's spawn point, turn right and follow the perimeter walkway to reach this area. During Turf War, opponents can't swim up to this ledge on your team's side of the map—if they want to flank you, they have to go all the way around. But in Splat Zones, the wall beneath this perch can be inked. So watch for opponents traveling through this area. Placing an Ink Mine or Splash Wall at the top of the ledge is a good deterrent.

C By turning left out of your team's spawn point and following the perimeter path, you can access a long, narrow corridor leading to this central overwatch position. Like the previous location, this spot is ideal for covering the center, making it a popular sniper perch. Step out onto the mesh grate for a better view of the middle. But be ready to duck back into the adjoining corridor if you come under fire—retreat and hide in your own ink to recover and replenish your ink-tank. The corridor is also a good spot for Squid Beakons, giving your team quick access to the stage's center. But the glass floor sections of this corridor can't be inked. Take this into account when swimming here, jumping over each glass section to maintain your forward momentum.

Recommended Weapons

Splattershot Jr.

Any rapid-firing weapon works well here as many engagements occur at close range while you round the stage's twisting corridors. The Splattershot Jr.'s high rate of fire and wide spread make it a well-rounded choice for any game mode.

Splat Charger

When positioned on the central sniper perches, Splat Charger and other charge weapons are great for picking off opponents in the low-lying center. You can even counter-snipe opponents on the surrounding ledges.

Splash Wall

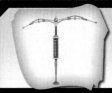

The stage's numerous narrow corridors make Splash Wall extremely useful on this stage. Use it to block enemy movement or to simply give yourself an advantage during duels.

Killer Wail

The central corridors in the middle of the stage are high-traffic areas. Use Killer Wail to target opponents in these cramped chokepoints.

TURF WAR

Urchin Underpass

In Turf War, rush to the center of the stage during the opening moments of the match. To reach the center quickest, head to the right side of the stage immediately after spawning, using the flanking path to fire down on the middle. Your opponents are likely to take the central path, passing through the narrow chokepoint in the middle—focus your fire on this area to ambush opponents as they rush into view. If your team can lock down the center early, make cautious advances into the opposing team's territory. Plant Squid Beacons along the elevated perches on your team's side of the map to maintain constant pressure in the center. If possible, take possession of the enemy team's flanking paths too. When there's one minute left in the match, glance at the GamePad's map to ensure your team's side of the stage is thoroughly inked. If not, have one teammate retreat from the center to apply touch-ups.

Legend

 Spawn Point

At the start of a match, don't worry too much about inking the area around your team's spawn point. Instead, make an aggressive push toward the stage's center. Establishing early control of the center can make all the difference, effectively trapping the opposing team on their side of the stage. But before the match ends, glance down at the GamePad and make sure the area around your team's spawn point is thoroughly inked. Chances are a teammate has already covered this area.

Be careful when operating around the horizontal nets stretched across these paths. Ink both sides of the net, then jump through the net in squid form to reach the other side of the path. If you don't ink the opposite side of the net, you may land in enemy ink, inflicting damage and slowing your advance. These nets can be a good place to ambush opponents. If enemies approach a net, ink the ground around the base so they land in your team's ink.

The fight for the stage's center is ongoing. Instead of rushing through the central corridor, use one of the perimeter perches to spread ink here. But watch out for opponents positioned on the other perches. If you don't have a long-range charger weapon, you may be at a disadvantage, unable to retaliate. Instead of trying to hit a distant sniper, fall back and attempt to flank your enemy.

SPLAT ZONES

Urchin Underpass

Legend

Spawn Point	— Splat Zone Boundary

There is only one Splat Zone on Urchin Underpass, located in the low-lying area in the stage's center. As in Turf War, waste no time rushing to the stage's center—head right from your spawn point and use the perimeter path to reach the Splat Zone before your opponents. In addition to capturing the Splat Zone, apply pressure on the central corridor as this is the path most likely traveled by your opponents. Defend the Splat Zone by occupying the perimeter corridor—head to the left when advancing from your team's spawn point. Here you can fire down on the Splat Zone and provide your team a forward spawn point with the use of Squid Beacons.

This elevated perch, just off the perimeter corridor, is great for covering the Splat Zone. Drop a Squid Beacon in the corridor and step out onto the grate to arc ink down onto the Splat Zone. From here you can also toss sub weapons, helping spread ink—Splat Bombs and Sprinklers are particularly effective. However, enemies can ink the wall just below this perch. So watch out for point-blank sneak attacks from below.

Beware of enemy Splash Walls. These are very effective for blocking access to the Splat Zone, particularly in the oft-travelled central corridor. Remember, you can't shoot through an opponent's Splash Wall, but they can shoot you. Instead of firing into an enemy Splash Wall, make a hasty retreat to avoid getting pelted by incoming fire.

The Splat Zone is somewhat protected by these low walls, making it difficult to thoroughly spread ink from a distance. If you don't have sub weapons like Splat Bombs, Burst Bombs, or Sprinklers, you may need to drop down into the zone and apply ink directly. But don't linger down here too long. Once captured, retreat to one of the perimeter perches and defend the zone from a safe distance, otherwise you're likely to be bombarded by incoming ink and explosive sub weapons.

WALLEYE WAREHOUSE

OVERVIEW

If you're new to multiplayer, Walleye Warehouse is a great stage to get acquainted with ink battles. The stage is relatively flat, with only a few elevated perches that can be used by snipers. This means you have more of a fighting chance, even if you're not the most experienced player. There are also no water features or steep, fatal drops, making Walleye Warehouse one of the more forgiving stages. Take some time getting familiar with the stage, learning the benefits of its flanking paths while using the crates for cover and concealment when engaging opponents in the chaotic center.

Key Locations

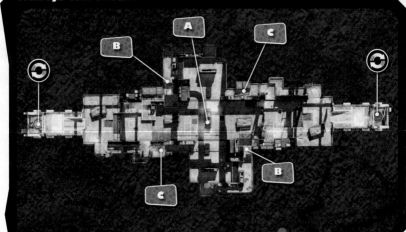

Walleye Warehouse

Legend

	Spawn Point
	Key Locations

Like most stages, controlling the center in Walleye Warehouse is essential for gaining an advantage. Make your stand near the large stack of crates in the middle and engage incoming opponents. Most opponents come charging down the middle, making it easy to pick them off with charge weapons, Killer

Wail, Inkzooka, and Seekers. But don't forget to cover the flanking paths too. Use the numerous crates to your advantage, by hiding behind them or standing on top for a height advantage. The shipping containers on the edges of this area, near each team's spawn point, are popular sniper perches, perfect for covering the center.

 Veer left out of your team's spawn point to access this elevated path leading toward the stage's center. The yellow and black barrier running along the ledge of this walkway makes it impossible for squid to swim up the walls, making this path relatively secure— opponents can only access this

area from your team's spawn area. This makes it easy to keep your team's path inked during Turf War. The path leads to three different mesh platforms, ideal for accessing the center of the stage. Advancing along this perimeter path is also ideal for sneaking up on opponents, especially if they're applying pressure on your team's spawn point.

 Turn right out of your team's spawn point to access this narrow perimeter path leading toward the stage's center. Unlike the other perimeter path, this one is only partially protected, noted by the yellow and black barriers along the ledge. Once you drop off this ledge, watch out for opponents below. The

adjoining path leads toward the center, but be careful when entering the narrow corridor. This area is often watched by enemy snipers. Keep this corridor coated in your team's ink and swim through to avoid getting picked off by opponents. If you suspect opponents are camped here, lead the way with a Seeker and swim behind it.

Recommended Weapons

Splattershot Jr.

Any of the rapid-firing Splattershot weapons work well here. But when it comes to Turf War, it's hard to top the ink-spreading mastery of the Splattershot Jr.

Krak-On Splat Roller

The flat surfaces and narrow pathways make roller-based weapons very effective here. You can also hide in your ink behind crates (or the tarp-covered ramps) and whack passing opponents with your roller.

Splat Bombs

Whether lobbing these explosives down range or bouncing them around tight corners, Splat Bombs are a great option for spreading ink or taking out opponents.

Echolocator

Given the numerous hiding spots on this stage, using Echolocator is great for keeping tabs on your opponents, helping you avoid enemy ambushes. Killer Wail is also very effective when aimed down the congested center of the stage.

TURF WAR

Walleye Warehouse

Legend

 Spawn Point

In Turf War, before making a push for the center, be sure to thoroughly ink your team's side of the stage. This means inking the area around your team's spawn point as well as the perimeter paths. The elevated path to the left of your spawn point is particularly important. Since this area is rarely accessed by the enemy, you'll probably only

need to make one pass here. This path also offers the safest access to the center of the stage. Instead of getting bogged down in the center, look for opportunities to flank your opponents, particularly by pressuring their perimeter hallway and central ramps. As the match approaches its final seconds, use specials like Inkzooka and Inkstrike to expand your ink coverage on the opposing team's side of the stage.

The shipping containers are covered with black tarps and can't absorb ink, but you can ink the sheets of plywood on top of a few shipping containers. Not only does this give your team some extra ink coverage, but it also allows you to quickly swim across the tops of these containers without being noticed. Or simply hide in your ink atop these shipping containers and ambush your opponents. The two shipping containers in the middle serve as excellent sniper perches.

There are four ramps on this stage covered with black tarps—one near each spawn point and two near the center. As a result, you can't ink these ramps. So when swimming in squid form, it's best to avoid these areas. These can also be good spots to ambush your opponents—with no ink at their feet, they won't be able to swim away. Avoid getting bogged down at these chokepoints as there's never a shortage of incoming ink or Splat Bombs.

Don't be afraid to make pushes into enemy territory. This perimeter corridor offers a great path for pushing behind your opponents and inking territory near their spawn point. But don't expect them to give up this corridor without a fight. Activate Bubbler or Kraken before making your advance and attack aggressively. Alternatively, use charge weapons and Seekers to help secure this narrow hall.

SPLAT ZONES

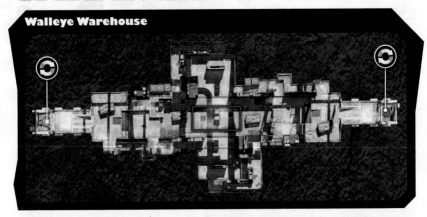

Walleye Warehouse

Legend

⊕ Spawn Point	— Splat Zone Boundary

On Walleye Warehouse there is only one Splat Zone, located in the center of the stage. At the start of the match, make a quick push to the middle by using the central path leading out of your team's spawn point. The Splat Zone is rather large, with a wall of crates stacked

in the center—you must coat the entire zone with your ink, so don't get comfortable hiding behind that wall of crates. As the match progresses, avoid using the central path to reach the Splat Zone. Instead, turn left out of your team's spawn point and use the elevated flanking path to sneak up on the Splat Zone. Drop a Squid Beakon along this path to give your team a safe spawn area near the Splat Zone.

Expect a chaotic fight in the center of the stage during the opening moments of the match. The stack of crates in the center of the Splat Zone acts like a wall, dividing two halves of the zone. Ink your team's side of the zone, then toss Splat Bombs or Suction Bombs over the low center crate to ink the other side. You can also arc ink over this gap in the wall to spread ink on the other side. This is often safer than side stepping around the wall, where you'll likely be exposed to direct fire.

Once your team has captured the Splat Zone, apply pressure on the enemy's central ramps. Use linear attacks like Seekers, Killer Wail, and Inkzooka to ambush opponents as they rush down the ramps covered in black tarps. In addition to inking the Splat Zone, work on inking the entire center of the warehouse to prevent your opponents from gaining easy access. Forcing them to ink a path toward the Splat Zone will eat up precious time, extending the duration of your team's control.

Beware of the impending Inkstrike. This special is extremely effective, potentially capturing the entire Splat Zone on its own. So when defending the Splat Zone, provide coverage from the perimeter to avoid getting caught up in a devastating Inkstrike. By hiding in your ink along the perimeter, you can monitor enemy traffic and respond before they can capture the zone.

Tip

Want to reach the center of the warehouse quickly? Toss a Seeker down from your spawn point and swim through its ink to reach the Splat Zone before your opponents. Charge weapons are also great for creating long, narrow trails of ink toward the center.

COMING SOON!

Stay tuned to *Splatoon* for more incoming content, including new ink battle stages, game modes, weapons, and gear. Here's a sneak peek at a few of the new features you can look forward to.

STAGES

Bluefin Depot

Kelp Dome

Camp Triggerfish

Port Mackerel

GAME MODE: TOWER CONTROL

WEAPONS

Carbon Roller

Custom E-Liter 3K

N-Zap85

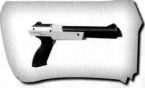

E-Liter 3K Scope

N-Zap89

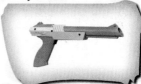

Inkbrush

Rapid Blaster Deco

L-3 Nozzlenose

Splash-o-matic

212

PLAYERS
Grow Up Progression

School Uniforms

Armor

Squid Form

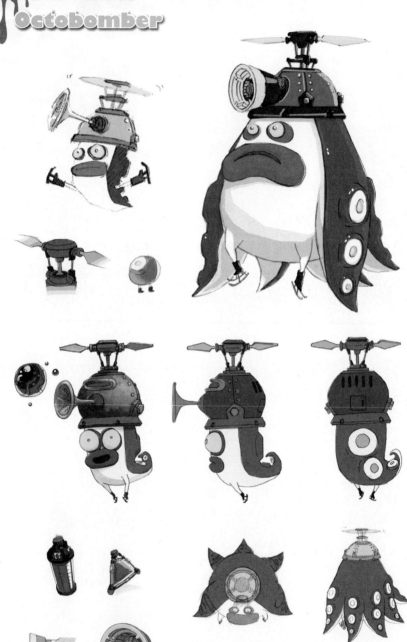

Octotrooper

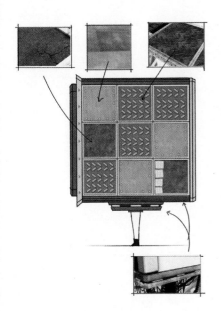

Octonozzle

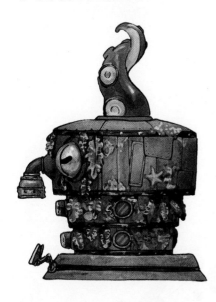

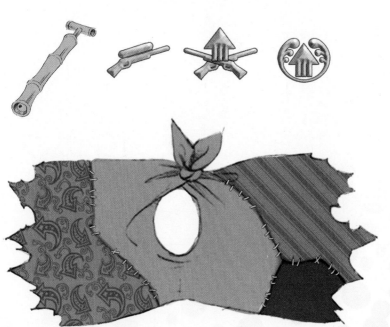

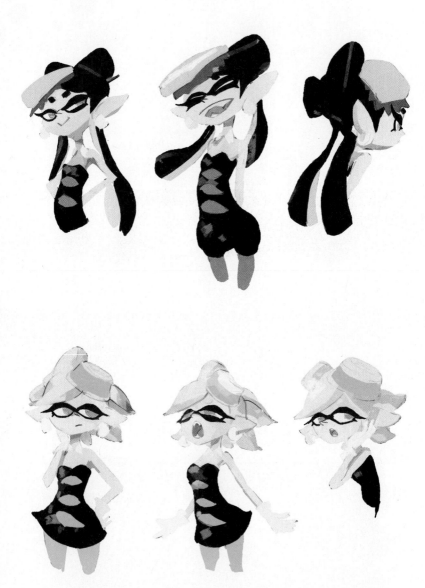

Sheldon

Annie

Crusty Sean

WEAPONS

Main

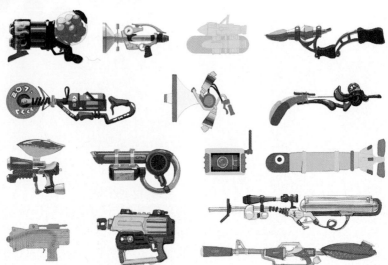

Sub

.52 Gal

Kettle

Playground

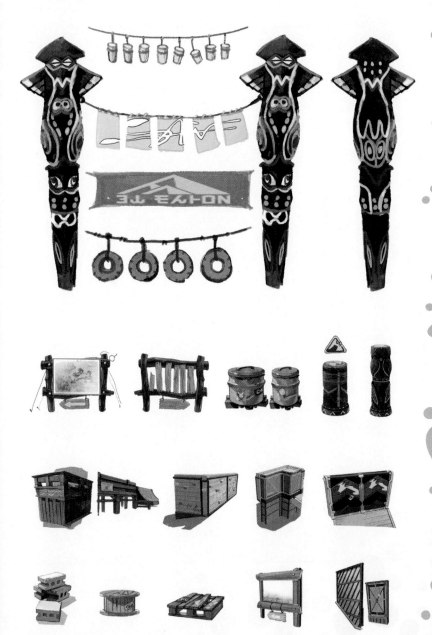

OBJECTS
Road

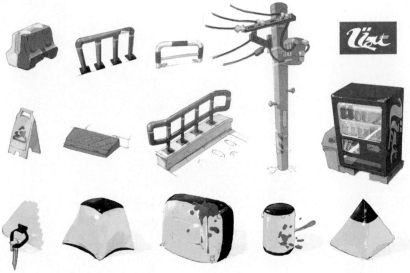

Greenhouse

Solo Mode

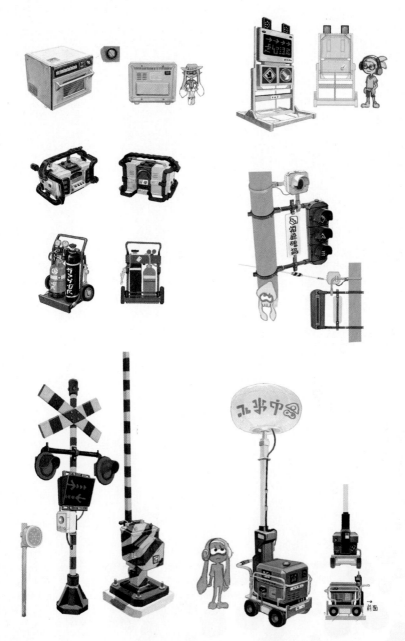

ENVIRONMENTS
Landscape

Octo Valley

Octarian Stage

Octarian Stage

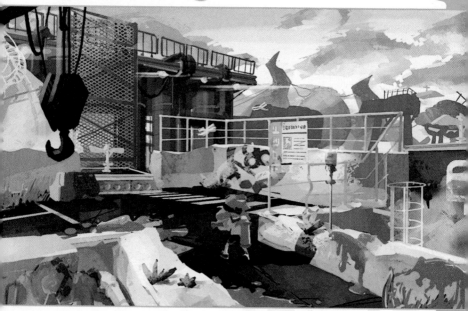

ENVIRONMENTS
Highway

Parking

Playground

Suburb

Official Game Guide
Written by David Knight

Prima Games
An imprint of Random House, LLC,
a Penguin Random House Company
3000 Lava Ridge Courte, Ste. 100
Roseville, CA 95661

www.primagames.com

ISBN: 978-1-1018-9850-5

Prima Games has made every effort to determine that the information contained in this book is accurate. However, the publisher makes no warranty, either expressed or implied, as to the accuracy, effectiveness, or completeness of the material of this book. The publisher cannot provide any additional information or support regarding gameplay, hints and strategies, or problems with hardware or software. Such questions should be directed to the support numbers provided by the game and/or device manufacturers as set forth in their documentation. Some game tricks require precise timing and may require repeated attempts before the desired result is achieved.

PRIMA GAMES STAFF

VP and Publisher
Mike Degler

Licensing Managers
Aaron Lockhart
Christian Sumner

Digital Publishing Manager
Tim Cox

Marketing Manager
Katie Hemlock

Operations Manager
Stacey Beheler

CREDITS

Product Manager
Jesse Anderson

Designer
Jeff Weissenberger

Production Designer
Julie Clark

Copy Editor
Julia Mascardo

SPECIAL THANKS

Prima Games would like to thank Emiko Ohmori, Taylor Stockton, Kanani Kemp, Takashi Tomizuka, Robert Johnson, Santavorn Mam, Eric Compton, Robert Ward, Max Reddie, Bobby Badeaux, Geoffery Cox, Kelly Eggers, Andrew Bendokas, Ethan Stockton, Morgan Ritchie, Daniel Orihuela, Corey Olcsvary, James Sakshaug, Doug Dorning, Dan Simpson, Ben Ong and Tasha Ramage for their help and support.